HOW TO BE
AND STAY SEXY

FOURTH EDITION

ALLANA PRATT

INTIMACY EXPERT

TABLE OF CONTENTS

INTRODUCTION

BEING EXACTLY WHO YOU ARE

Some of you may know me from years ago on Leeza Live as the Sexy Mom Expert. Yes, that was Source's way of helping me pick myself up after my dark night of the soul. Now most people know me as an Intimacy Expert and Relationship Coach helping men, women and couples heal from heartbreak and live unapologetically. And with the launch of the **HeartMates Dating App and Intimacy Training** all rolled into one … others will now see me supporting singles to Become The One To Find the One … so they Keep the One!

I'm still a small town Canadian girl, 'Mum' to my now 17 year old son, fiercely loving and tender coach to my clients, customers, and community, and patient, compassionate cheerleader to Little Allana within me. The qualities that have emerged in me are true of any woman embracing her feminine power. I know our core relationship is with the Divine itself.

We are here to heal our relationship with ourselves, embrace our partnership with Source and then that internal communion effortlessly ripples into a healthier, more satisfying and profoundly connected relationship with a beloved.

As I've evolved over the decades and healed my own heart, my love for all people has grown into a Soup of Oneness.

Unconditional Love. Zero judgment. In How To Be and Stay Sexy, which I wrote in its original edition a decade ago, I refer to binary terms of woman or man, male or female. Please know I am inclusive of All people, regardless of sexual orientation, gender identity, disabilities, or color of skin, we ALL have the right to be respected, appreciated and welcomed to Become the One To Find the One ... We Are All ONE.

We're ALL stardust. The average human has trillions of cells, made of quadrillions of atoms, originating in the stars. We are galactic beings, the very structures that make up our bodies come from across the galaxy.

We all experience anxiety, depression, overwhelm, stress, and fears ... And we all possess intelligence, awareness, discernment, and intuition when our minds and hearts are brought into unity and alignment.

As ANY human being of any sexual orientation, gender identity, life circumstance, or past trauma does the "inner work", they achieve inner balance, a state of Grace where innate wisdom guides what I call HeartMates towards one another ... so please, if you would be so gracious, if you are a part of my cherished LGBTQ+ community reading this book, please receive my binary words through the lens of how you choose to honor yourself.

The same applies to the way I use a variety of terms such as God, Goddess, The Divine, the Universe, Higher Power, Source, and the Field to represent the many ways people identify and connect to a power greater than ourselves, yet within ourselves. I do so to honor, include, and respect everyone's point of view while doing my best to write authentically.

So here we go with my expression of feminine energy ... my definition of a woman who embodies the Light of Source:

a woman who is **sacredly sexy,**

fiercely loves herself exactly as she is,

courageously tells the truth with bold kindness,

is at peace in every inch of her awesomely aging skin,

turns heads when she enters the room from her **magnetic inner glow,**

gives herself **permission** to rejoice in her sexuality, her body, her heartfelt self-expression,

sees other sexy moms as sisters and **celebrates** them,

knows **asking for help** is wise and makes life run more smoothly,

says **"no" when she means "no"** and "yes" when she means "yes",

speaks to herself with kind, **compassionate,** loving, sultry devotion,

defines her **true core wisdom** as the Sacred Feminine, the Divine Mother, and Radiance Itself.

"I feel sexy when I breath deep into my pelvis, soften my gaze, expand my awareness, appreciate the world around me and softly smile on the inside, knowing I have the capacity to experience reverence, humility, and limitless pleasure at any moment I choose."

- me, back when I was 41 years old

(note about this photo: This was taken at the end of a regular headshot photo shoot. I believe every woman ought to enjoy a sexy photo shoot and explore your flavors of the feminine, touch your depth, stretch your edges, let go ...)

I am absolutely humbled with gratitude for the privilege of sharing my wisdom and experiences with you. My journey has been one of ups and downs. I imagine yours has been much the same. It has been my courage to learn to love and celebrate myself no matter what that has kept me going and now gives me the honor of sharing with you what has worked for me, and what has helped all those I've touched thus far.

And while I feel that I was born to do the work I'm doing now, I was "bred" to do something very different. You see, I started working with my father in his pharmacy, being groomed to take over the store. The customers loved me, I did a good job, my dad was so proud, but I hated it. From that experience I alchemized the lesson that I love people and decided to find a better fit in a new line of work. I decided to be a professional model and dancer. (Yes, my parents freaked! xox) I had danced ballet, jazz, and tap as a child and I thought it would be fun to travel the world on cruise lines. Mom and Dad had a royal conniption. But I went for it anyway, hopping on my Uncle Phil's 18-wheeler to make it in Hollywood, and ended up landing a gig in Tokyo which expanded into international modeling, acting, being a spokesperson, and an interviewer.

How does one find the courage to follow their heart, know when to let go of something good and make room for great, incorporate the lessons from each stage, and keep expanding -- all the while not living for tomorrow, rather, savoring today?

I think it comes down to asking:

WHAT IS YOUR WHY?

Here's the deal. Some days I am unstoppable and other days I am scared and literally curl into the fetal position on the floor and cry. Other days I am pissy, and still others I am overflowing with gratitude and wonder. The only thing that seems to keep me afloat, regardless of my humanness and responding to the challenges the universe deals to me is a "WHY" that's bigger than my considerations.

Why did I leave a secure future taking over the pharmacy?

Why did I ride an 18-wheeler down to LA?

Why did I move to Tokyo?

Why did I divorce the multimillionaire first husband?

Why did I divorce the second husband and become a single, motherless mom of an infant?

The list goes on. Why?

Because I KNOW there's more.

Because I FEEL that more pulling me.

Because I'm willing to forgive myself for my mistakes and MOVE ON.

Because I am quite clear that I don't want to wake up one day in heaven and not have given it my best shot. I don't want to barely be able to look myself in the mirror one day because I've sold out, I've given up, I've played it safe, or because I was too afraid to go for my dream.

That's why I responsibly yet courageously find a way to live my passions in my career. While I don't model anymore, I still "perform", and get that timeless, in-the-zone feeling of being on set, interacting with the whole crew like a family when I interview someone, or give my expertise on TV or radio. I even lose track of time and feel used by Spirit when I speak to an intimate group of moms, or a large auditorium filled with burned-out business women.

Your WHY has to be bigger than the frustrations of life.

And here's the cool thing. Imagine for a moment that YOU are the Universe. You are God. You are Goddess, looking at the rest of us on Earth. You see someone who's not sure how to work it all out, but is trying to incorporate their passion into life, into their work, into their hobby. You see that person as a spark, a bright light illuminating on the screen of Mother Gaia.

It's as if you perk up and say, "Hey, we have a LIVE one, here!" If you were the Universe, wouldn't you want to support someone who's going for it?

I swear that's what's happened to me in my life. Whenever I SHOW UP, my dreams or something better always comes through. Quite often Plan B is better than I could ever have imagined on my own.

Be willing to give up good for great. Be willing to cultivate your will, your intention and then surrender, let go and see what the tide brings in. Get yourself a really good WHY that will take you through the mundane as well as the challenges.

So, what's my WHY?

You are!!!

It makes me cry "happy tears" when I see a woman claim her feminine power and juiciness! I love seeing a woman let go of the constrictions in her heart and magnificently exude a radiance that can stop traffic. And it's not from "trying" -- it's from stopping the "trying" and softening into the truth that she's enough.

Thank YOU for being my WHY.

I am committed to healing the feminine and redefining sexy. I am here to guide you to embody Spirit in your life because we don't have to exhaust ourselves doing life alone. I am here to inspire all women to feel their innate radiance, empower them to feel the power that comes from their heart, guide women to enjoy the most fulfilling, luscious, profound relationships with themselves and thus, with their partners. I do this so we all shine fully, savoring the pleasures of this world, fiercely loving ourselves and as a result, every being we encounter.

The feminine (which is in men as well) is allowing, receiving, balancing, and possessing divine union internally that will

VII • ALLANA PRATT

be mirrored externally, and YOU are officially part of this transformation by reading this book and gifting yourself with your full sensual and sexual expression.

And may this permission to soften, open, and trust bring you more peace, success and ease than you currently experience. I celebrate you!!!

While I encourage you to read the whole book … I invite you to also breathe it into your cells. This book is energy, truth, carrying with it the life force chi to awaken dormant superpowers within you, to heal wounds in your heart, to ignite your evolutionary spark.

Let it MOVE YOU.

Let's get real with the obstacles, limiting beliefs, societal bullshit, and authentically painful life experiences we've all been through regarding our sexuality, our light, our feminine power.

I gathered the statements below from clients over the years. These are things clients said when they first came to heal from the past, drop into their heart, step into their glory, find the one, or ignite their marriage when they worked with me privately, in group or my HeartMates Intimacy Training as a single woman, or as a couple.

- *Being sexy, flirty, and soft seems so weak. I've worked hard for my success and want to be valued for my accomplishments and not just my beauty.*

- *You talk so fluffy like a floozie. Great for masculine attention, yet I highly doubt men respect you. Yet I will admit men tell me I intimidate them.*

- *Letting a man see me sweat scares me. I know I only show him my perfect side. yet I'm scared to be taken advantage of and hate feeling vulnerable.*

- *Letting go of my goals, letting go of control, letting go and doing these sensual practices you speak of seems stupid, yet when I tried them, they actually made me feel panicked. I don't want to let go of control and be open to abuse.*

- *I've never valued my femininity, was told to "man up" even as a little girl, to do things myself, to never need a man, and while I admit I'm jealous of women who are sexy, honestly, I don't respect them either. Weak woman letting him open the door. What is she, useless?*

- *How do you honestly do these practices when working sixty to eighty hours a week? I don't get paid to relax. I get acknowledged and praised and paid to work.*

- *My husband is never stepping up, never following through, never keeping his word on a regular basis. I have to do everything and I'm exhausted, resentful and want to leave him.*

Did any of these statements from my clients resonate with you?

Write in the space below what YOUR biggest challenge, obstacle, limiting belief, problem, stuck'ness, or pain in your heart truly is.

Ask yourself: what's stopping you from embodying your Divine Sacred Sexual Feminine Power and Radiance?

_____
_____
_____
_____
_____
_____
_____
_____
_____

Thank you.

So here's the deal. What happened DID happen. And it hurts. And I'm sorry. So sorry. And the beliefs, protection mechanisms, and survival patterns have worked to keep you safe'ish, secure'ish and happy'ish. Yes?

I'm not interested in getting rid of any part of you. Remember the title of this Introduction - **Being Exactly As You Are.** This book is about lovingly and bravely scooping up our afraid parts, angry parts, ashamed parts, wobbly parts ... and integrating them into your new present moment superpower.

No sprinkles on top of the ice cream cone of shit here. No spiritual bypassing here!

We're going to literally become alchemical priestesses to turn fear into confidence, pain into potency, sadness into compassion, control freakness into discerning awareness, hopelessness into sacred surrender. We are becoming Whole. Home. One with All.

I've got you.

And I love you.

Let's begin.

CHAPTER 1

FACING SHAME

I'm writing to you, my beloved sister, in this new edition of *How to Be and Stay Sexy*, feeling like I've been reborn, as if I've emerged from a cocoon I didn't know I was in.

Blindspots? I had them, yet I was convinced I had it all together. Now I can shine the light on the blindspots of others so effortlessly. I attribute that to having discovered and dealt with my own first.

I am writing to you now in my power as a seer, healer, and spiritual guide; as a more authentic, grateful, fully self-expressed woman. I'm humbled, broken to the core, separated from all that kept me in the illusion of safety. I'm putting the puzzle pieces together in a new dimension of feminine power that had been calling to me all along ... and I was perhaps a six out of ten in cultivating it ... and am now entering level seven, eight ... mature, quieter, more surrendered and yet one hundred times more badass, connected, and powerful.

Many factors were in the way of my growth. Shame was the first.

I was ashamed of many things ... not having a workable relationship with my ex-husband yet encouraging you to find your beloved. I felt shame for being single and not happily married, being successful yet not dripping in millions, and finally, I felt guilty about being attractive and teaching women of all shapes, sizes, ages, and cultures about being sexy.

This voice in my head kept saying, "Who do you think you are?" or "Oh, if they only knew the truth, Allana!"

I wasn't aware of any authentic behaviors, just my fired up excitement to serve, to shine, and to empower. I had no idea I was overcompensating, using over-the-top gestures and adjectives ad nauseam. I was so blind to the shame that I felt quite real, true, and passionate about my mission.

While I'm clear now that I provide great value, that I am a master communicator, an art history major, and that I love using words like delicious and luscious, in hindsight I can see that I was adding JUST one more thing to ensure you REALLY knew that I loved you, to impress upon you that I was sincere.

I was afraid to simply claim, own, and move beyond my relationship situation, financial reality and physical appearance and shine – Source – from the inside out as I preached. Deep reflection has taught me that I was afraid that you wouldn't believe me if I told you the whole truth, so I taught you the depth and truth of what I knew for your highest good and left it at that.

Yet, I should have remembered the adage - be careful what you wish for. I learned that to serve *your* highest good is only possible when I am living *my* highest good.

I know now that life fell apart so I could reassemble on higher ground.

A long time ago, the first onslaught of life lessons came when my son jumped out of his dad's truck before it came to a stop, his foot was run over, and broken, and I was enraged. To make matters worse, my ex blamed our son and I completely lost it. While I'm certain I was rolling eyes and sighing heavily already, at that moment I really let 'er rip and said just how furious I was with his dad. My son responded protectively, supporting his dad and told me he never wanted to see me again. He moved in with his father.

Crushed, in reactionary despair, in my vulnerable, open fashion I wrote about it in my newsletter and I manifested my fear … hundreds opted out of my newsletter, some responding in anger that I was a fraud, teaching about empowered relationships when mine were a wreck.

I needed a miracle.

I was on my knees, humbled.

Ask and you shall receive.

When two separate friends mentioned the same spiritual guide in the same day, I called. She told me this had nothing to do with my son's father and everything to do with me causing drama instead of moving forward powerfully in my purpose. Smack.

I was awake.

She told me I was operating at 8 to 10 % of my power, draining it all, watching for his next wrong move, and that in time, he would become my biggest support.

("You've got to be kidding me," was my reply to that one.)

She told me this self-created drama was in the way, stopping me from attracting my beloved, taking my business from stressed to making good money into calmness with having such abundance that I'd never think about money again, only service to the planet.

She insisted that all I learn I share with you, my beloved community, to make each micro-conversation my focus, forget about building my database or being on television. She taught me that each moment contained the whole Universe. She said that I am here to serve women and children, and told me that working with men has prepared me to heal personally, and that it is beneficial to teach my "man whisperer" practices to awaken a man's deepest nobility.

As our work progressed, she was able to show me how to see past the veils of someone's anger, underneath to the core of their emotions.

I saw my son's father as a little boy, not unlike my scared inner little girl, wanting to be safe and liked. His was saying, "Why did you leave me?" And even deeper, "Why weren't you there for me the way I needed you?" to his mother. From this perspective I could see that watching for his next wrong move MADE him make a wrong move! He was walking on the egg shells I had strewn on the ground! I was contributing to him letting me down! Then I saw the frustration that he wanted to take out on me, yet couldn't because I'd ignore him, so he'd taken it out on our son. I was adding to my son's suffering. I nearly vomited.

I could see how focusing on praising his inner little boy with respectful mannerisms suitable for adults could shift things. I began to point out all the things that have happened for the good due to his focus, interests, talents, and follow-through. I began praising him to our son, including his father in nightly "thank you's," which I had never done before.

Within two weeks he called to say, "Let's put the past behind us. Whatever I need to do to have us on the same page I'm willing to do it. Gabe is playing us against one another and we need to unite and create an amazing life for our boy."

Holy shit.

I could barely take it in.

My ego resisted and I wanted him to apologize.

My mentor compassionately yet firmly laughed in my face. "Grow up," she said. "Peace is our objective, not righteousness."

For a period of time, he was my biggest support, praising ME, standing by his word, still hiding some things from me, probably dreading that I'd attack him, and while he wasn't perfect, when he was met by grounded praise, understanding and cooperation, even his questionable behaviors were dissolving. And if I needed to handle something, I still had mediation. Yet I didn't focus on that anymore. I just knew it was there. Instead, I focused on the fact that he even paid for a full-day intensive with a child specialist one month for the whole family to attend.

What I never had growing up -- a family of respect, connection, listening and safety, was unfolding.

AND of course, I can hear you, have things stayed the same? No ... and yes. Our son has created the peace he needed by living with his dad. His dad hasn't spoken to me for many years. Everything is peaceful. Not the perfect motherhood I dreamed of. Yet overflowing with lessons of allowance, surrender, compassion, and still ripe with possibility for the future.

And did things also shift with my own father?

My spiritual consultant said there was no room for conflict for one who is living their purpose. Drains will not do. And so after not talking to my father for years and our last conversation being so abusive, again I was able to see past the veils of his behavior to his deeper emotions. "Why didn't you take over the business that I groomed for you? Why did you leave and go so far away? Why are you struggling so much? Just come home and be safe and responsible."

Wow. He didn't hate me, he just wanted to protect me.

So I wrote a card telling him how much I appreciated the foundation he built for me, thanking him for teaching me so much about building a business because now I'm running one. What I didn't tell him, but did say to his soul, was that although he is now dry, his drug and alcohol abuse taught me about how devastating it can be to grow up not being safe, seen, validated, or heard. He's helped me end a cycle of running from problems by learning to face them and heal them.

Then he called.

Nothing had changed. His wife still finished his sentences. He was still negative, in pain, in drama, even depressed. What changed is that I didn't pipe in after two minutes with "Can I talk to my dad please without you finishing his sentences?" I just listened, breathed and got my dad. What changed is that in my super-duper positive coach guru talk, I didn't try to make him see the positive side, I didn't try to make him do some visualizations or affirmations or let go of the draining people ... I listened, breathed and got my dad.

And even though I didn't connect with him the way I'd hoped, and even though he didn't hear me, validate me, celebrate me, or acknowledge me, I felt so full I didn't need it.

All I knew was that I loved my dad.

And I love my son's father. I'm not IN love with him because that sacred contract is done, but I love and appreciate him supporting our son's life.

My need to be right is falling away.

My need for recognition to be enough is gone.

My need for you to approve of me seems like a lifetime ago.

My concern about having things all figured out is dying too.

I'm settling into a more mature deliciousness, a quieter sultriness, a more reverent humility with Source, a more understated yet massively more expansive honoring of my worth and my power.

It's spilling into my private sessions in laser-sharp, firm, loving insights. It's igniting my role as the sensual, spiritual Barbara Walters sharing profound interviews with the world about true feminine power, and true embodiment of spirit.

I'm letting go of the struggle of being an entrepreneur and embracing my badass business woman who contributes to humanity with the HeartMates Dating App, thriving Intimacy Breakthrough Group and Inner Circle Coaching programs, a team of amazing Allana Pratt Certified Coaches, a glorious Intimacy Success Advisor who welcomes new clients for me giving me time to inspire more with publicity, podcasts and summits and cultivate investors for the app's success.

I am embracing myself as a Queen, practicing grounded, unwavering faith in my own self to create a life of peace, pleasure, and profound service.

I'm in a new-found balance, with my own veils removed, living in my own spiritual backyard, and I'm healed, the mechanism of overcompensating to be good enough has dissolved (although I still overdeliver with clients and love to send my staff goodies, xox). I'm more approachable, authentic, inviting, and effective at sharing exactly how we women can be balanced in our feminine and masculine energies. Not hardened, cold, bitchy, or dry. Nor over-the-top, too much, or fluffy -- right in the sweet spot of true feminine power where we are light-hearted because we are vessels of light itself, free of blocks, neither over nor under compensating, and fully in the present -- safe, open, empowered, and free.

So to review, here's how to turn things around with your ex, your father, the father of your kids, or anyone that's pissing you off:

1. Acknowledge you need help and wisely receive support.

2. Soften your heart, your view, and see beyond the personal veils to the core emotion of the individual.

3. Trust your instincts and intuition. What do you hear, see, know, and feel to be true when you put yourself in their shoes?

4. Where are they actually YOU? (Take a breath ... I know that's hard to feel) Where do you behave the same way either physically, mentally, emotionally, spiritually, vocationally, financially, socially, parentally, romantically, or sexually with others? With yourself?

5. What negative outcomes can you take full responsibility for contributing to? Where did you leave your heart, react versus respond, assume versus ask questions, or continue an old sabotaging pattern?
Breathe.

6. Forgive yourself and forgive them. Journal, have rituals with candles, or speak with a coach. Write out several times, Thank you 'forgiving' me that experience as now I see, I've learned, I'm more aware, I'm grateful to have realized ...

7. Where are you actually stronger, more resilient, aware, forgiving, communicative, brave, or surrendered having gone through that experience? Can you even thank them in your prayers and meditation for awakening the best in you?

8. From compassion, understanding and courage, what is the most loving form of communication you can begin making with your Self, with Them?

9. Look for all the areas you can clean up your communication, with peripheral people, and with your expectations. Release all evidence that keeps the old paradigm in place. Release the story. Release that old identity of being a victim to your circumstances. Take your power back and embody all the lessons.

10. Enjoy the peace, freedom, and higher-ground consciousness you get to soar into, proud of the deep work you've done to get you here.

11. Acknowledge the healing you have gifted yourself and your ancestors and children with. We are all one, and ALL is different forever because of your work.

Congratulations brave sister.

CHAPTER 2

MAN WHISPERER

Another reason I was able to heal so quickly and powerfully with my son's father and my own father was the fact that I've coached over a hundred men and now coach couples regularly.

It's so humbling (and hysterical) because whenever I need to learn something, God always provides lessons. Like when I first became a mom I was hired to interview three parenting experts in a row. Hello?

Life graced me with a huge interview opportunity with David DeAngelo of Double Your Dating and since then I have been able to help men get out of their spinning heads, stop their hesitancy, heal their wounded hearts, cure "nice guy" and stay grounded, centered and heart-connected while claiming and ravishing a woman to the core of her soul.

I've surprisingly become somewhat of a Man Whisperer. They tell me things they haven't told anyone in their entire life. They say they feel safe, that they can feel I believe in men, that I can awaken the best in their heart. It's humbling and so rich.

- I've learned many secrets I want to share with you, about today's man who is looking for a relationship. Many men have not been unconditionally loved EVER. Someone in their past who was doing their best but was unconscious didn't see them, hear them, value them, or pay attention to them. Deep inside many question their worth and overcompensate with money, bravado, or on the other hand, don't come up to you when they really do like you, for fear of rejection. (What's curious here is that they are no different than us in this respect, yes?)

• Many men are empty inside, looking for validation on the outside and giving away their power to us, to our opinion of them. This makes them check out, not be present, forget things, watch another pretty woman go by. This ISN'T because they aren't into us! This is because they care about us the MOST and are afraid we won't approve of them, so they spin away in fear. (Again, pretty familiar story, yes? So, let this soften your old beliefs and open your heart.)

• Many men carry a lot of shame about their sexuality, thinking they are bad for wanting sex. This shame unhealed makes them look at us like pieces of meat or watch porn instead of facing their shame, healing it and learning more from sacred tantra classes or sexologists to teach them how to please us. They want nothing more than to give us pleasure and simply haven't been taught that it's possible to penetrate us with their eyes, their hearts, and their genitals. Yet they are quick learners! (Isn't this curious? What looks like shallowness is really shame? Deep inside they DO have noble hearts that want to honor us like a queen, I promise.)

• Men are almost speechless in the presence of our beauty. AND they have a wide variety of preferences for beauty. It's in the softness of our skin, the movement of our hips, the way the sun hits out hair, and the way our eyes sparkle. They are mesmerized with our confidence in the unknown and our peace in our bodies, less impressed with our accomplishments yet attracted to our capacity to do what makes us happy. (Please get that they are literally awestruck by our femininity, and our radiance. It awakens something nothing else in the world can awaken within them.)

- Men love that we have solid opinions, minds of our own, assurance in our values, and yet many complain we won't let them lead. They give examples like we need to rebut every comment they make like a debate, or that we won't accept their lead on where to go for dinner, or we only appreciate them for what they buy us versus acknowledge their thoughtfulness or listening. They are often intimidated by super successful women who they say feel as (or more) competitive than their guy friends even if we're pretty or hot. They may want to fuck us and leave, but not claim our hearts. (One man put it this way ... a powerful woman knows when to speak up and when to let it go.)

- Across the board men want us to be able to soften, and believe me, they don't see that as weak. These men letting me in to coach their wounded hearts took massive courage and they appreciate that it takes courage to let go of control and trust a man. They don't want us to be bumps on a log, of course. They want us to be WAY more expressive in our appreciation or even our preference for something else ... they complain they can't read us, that they wish we'd be WAY more honest and straight.

- Several men have stories of women doing no-shows on dates, or after a date saying they'd like to see them again and yet never returning calls or emails. This gives us women a bad rap! If he's not the one, kindly say something like, "I've enjoyed myself very much tonight and want to thank you for all you provided. I am not feeling we're a match and I wouldn't want to be in the way of you finding your beloved, so thank you for this experience and I wish you all the best." Truth honors them. Lies emasculate them, telling them they're so weak they couldn't handle the truth, when in fact, I believe it's US who can sometimes be weak, not facing our discomfort and ignoring a soul.

- Men complain that many women don't give them more than a coffee date to get to know them. They believe many of us in our power to create our world have passed by a really great guy who is reliable and kind because he's not a millionaire or a Brad Pitt look-alike. Many admit they are timid to be, as I say, "dark with heart" for many women have made them feel wrong for trying (ineffectively) to ravish them. But they REALLY want to please us, are willing to take kind, encouraging feedback, and MANY have buckets of love, attention, affection, appreciation, and adoration to shower on us. (Instead of giving up, compassionately guide him to the spa for some "man grooming" or let him know how happy it would make you if he joined you at a tantra class to understand a deeper way of connecting.)

- Many men don't understand that we want to be penetrated with their eyes, their heart AND their genitals and don't know how to be present, grounded, unwavering, and confident from the inside out. So use your feminine invitational temptress energy to invite him to make love to you with his eyes tonight or penetrate you with his heart through texts all day. Set him up to win so that you feel his solid banks of the river and can open your body as a gift to him, and for your own pleasure too! (Notice that YOU will also be trained here, to open past where you feel in control and this is HIS job to take you beyond your comfort zones, while holding you safe in his presence.)

- MANY men don't get that if they're not living their purpose and engaged in their passions that they aren't attractive, first of all, and secondly, they give away their power to us! Even though in our insecure moments we THINK we want to be number one, in reality, a man who puts us number one just gave up his direction, purpose, drive and legacy to us and he's wrapped around our little finger. The most effective relationships I've seen are when a man elegantly accomplishes his goals while his partner's encouraging love radiantly fuels his existence. He is grateful to his woman for her support, and showers her with appreciation. (This is so brilliant, for our man showering us with appreciation fills us to the brim to flow with Source energy to live OUR purpose with ease!)

- And lastly, if you do need to awaken his masculine energy to get his ass off the couch and live his purpose, being a bitch, a nag, or acting like his mother WON'T do it! You need to do YOUR work first! Let this valid anger at seeing him waste his gifts sink into your womb. Let it boil. Bring it up into your healed heart and let your truth transform verbally into fierce love. "I love you so f'ing much that I can't stand to see the world denied of your talents and gifts!" Or "I love you so madly that it hurts my heart to see you let your boss's opinion of you make you question your power. You are magnificent, now get out there and rock it honey!" Challenge him from love. Get beneath him with your radiance. Show him in your voice, your body, your eyes, your heart how much you believe in him and that it literally makes you ache to see him not engaged in his passions.

CHAPTER 3

THE HORSES

Oh, yes I've been a busy critter healing illusions and embodying direct connection with Source since the earlier editions of this book!

In fact, this next part is the precursor to a WHOLE new book that's unfolding. It's all about my humbling wake-up call to let go of control.

We all are coming to understand that our biggest challenges are our biggest gifts. That the betrayal, abuse and let downs of our early life become the very essence of what we're here to give.

Thus, we're here to teach what we're here to learn.

Yet facing our blindspots is not only challenging because we can't see the damn things, they're humbling as hell, bitter pills to swallow when we see how we've been sabotaging our happiness, success, peace and power the whole time in an effort to be free.

One of my teachers says to make art out of our kinks. Another says the healing of my greatest pain will be my greatest gift of service to the planet.

My teachers invite me to drop out of my survival mechanisms, release my ego, let go of the outcomes and simply speak my truth as an oracle, connected to Source. From the deep feminine perspective, I've been shown that most of us feminine light workers have been tortured, burned at the stake, had our heads chopped off in our past. For many of us, EVERYTHING in our lives has revolved around being safe, and so we must shift that, heal that, and embody Source or we keep creating situations that hurt us.

My whole life has revolved around feeling safe.

I was nice to be safe.

I worked hard to be safe.

I flirted with men to be safe.

I praised women to be safe.

I took on a business manager to be safe.

I eagle eye watched over my son's father to be safe.

I did affirmations and prayers to be safe.

I doused, muscle-tested and double-checked everything to be safe.

I looked to the outside for feedback, recognition, and agreement to be safe.

I stayed three steps ahead of everyone and everything to be safe.

And I was a fish in water, unable to see it because it's all I've known.

Years ago, one of my coaches gave me an assignment to ONLY ask myself, "What do I reeeeeally want to do right now?" I went into a panic.

I'm serious, sister, for twenty-four hours I was a mess -- crying, panicking, running circles around the back yard just breathing and saying logically, "Look! You're safe! You're alive! It's okay! You can ask, choose, create … it's okay!"

But there was a scared little girl's voice inside that said, "Never, ever, stop or we'll die!"

I realized I couldn't remember a time when I asked myself what I wanted to do. There had never been a time when I listened, trusted myself, took action, enjoyed the action, and celebrated having enjoyed my free will.

I learned that EVERY choice I'd made was focused on making sure I would look good, please someone, control the outcome -- SO I WOULD BE SAFE.

I had no idea what I really wanted. I had no idea who I really was. I had no idea how to trust myself.

And while I could say that I knew God loved me, I was definitely sure God was too busy to keep me safe. That was my job. Total distrust in God. Wow. Wake up call. Upon further analysis … I noticed that I had created little moments where I could surrender.

Coaching was first.

On my coaching forms when I'd begin a call I would always write GOD with big arms reaching up from the bottom of the page. I'd totally surrender, listen, channel like an oracle, see all blindspots with ease, love them fully, speak all these magnificent truths, transform lives, and then when the call was over … I'd go back to, "AH SHIT … how do I be safe?"

Dancing was second. Not so much alone, but definitely in class where my teacher was holding space, I was able to 100% let go, let Spirit have its way with my body, go on orgasmic rides of release, pleasure, depth, and empowerment without thinking a thought. Pure bliss, nourishing ease … but then I'd get back into the car … and think, "What do I need to do to be safe?"

Interviewing was third. Either interviewing another or being interviewed, again I trusted the container and felt filled by Source to either celebrate the depth of my guest's purpose or serve my audience sharing the flow of magical words pouring forth through me for another.

Motherhood was fourth. Not all of it, for he triggered me big time to provide safety for him – yet in the moments where I was present, when we used to dance on the coffee table, eat outside in the driveway or backyard by the fountain, catch balls and talk, and certainly at bedtime with rituals … I would leave my past/future spinning mind and sink into the present with him, into bliss, gratitude and fullness.

For many more years, the rest of my life still spun seeking safety … of course being with delicious girlfriends, moments of exquisite sex, and walks at sunset were lovely. There were moments yet I didn't see the prison bars through which these moments had to escape. This realization hit me square in the face when a spiritual consultant asked me to scan my body of all unfinished soul work, unfinished communications, broken promises, any lifetimes where I was unable to complete my dreams, and asked me some questions. What color was it? And where was it in/on my body? And what did it want?

I saw dirty orange welts all over my entire body. Deep, desperate grief welled up in my throat. I looked like a giraffe. We imagined a baby giraffe in front of me. It wanted compassion and freedom. I tenderly stroked it, calming it, validating its feelings, and then set it free into the wild. Then my spiritual consultant at the time asked me to imagine that I was holding on to the reins of horses, controlling them. How many were there? Two? Three? No, there were well over a hundred horses, symbols of all the unfinished, incomplete, thwarted, and crushed dreams. She said to send them compassion and grant them freedom. So I did. And I let go. And tears poured down my cheeks and a peace beyond words graced my body.

There's MORE, she said. Let metal chains and cuffs and links dissolve off me, walk forward in this wild field with the horses free, the giraffe free, and ME free. Give myself compassion and grant myself freedom, and I felt like a Native American priestess with hair like the manes of the horses approached, nuzzled me and left. I began to trust that what I needed would always arrive, what I no longer needed would pass, that I could trust the flow, I could trust me, I could trust God.

I humbly saw how tightly wound I was, shoulders in pain with knots, many dates yet haven't attracted the one, many separate stunning friends yet no "community" that drops in, wonderful business yet little downtime to enjoy, always something to do, all these horses to keep in control so I could be safe. Never creating the exhale. Always the inhale, inhale, inhale, so that I wouldn't risk being hurt.

As this process unfolded in my life, I began to trust what I want to do, what turned me on,

what I heard Source guiding me to do, and how I would best be utilized for the highest good of all. Today I have never felt more more fluid, free, balanced, humbled, surrendered, empowered, and unstoppable … such a range of deliciousness.

A great practice I use is to recognize when a fearful thought comes, to sit tall, breathe it into my open heart, exhale it away, releasing the constricted energy it holds, and simply being aware, listening to my breath. For me to not BE the thought, but recognize it, welcome it, release it and free the energy it is blocking. That is so empowering. Each time my head feels lighter. I no longer resist the fears!

Another life-changing and simplifying insight has been to notice ALL the intentions I had been making to be safe (more money, a man, thinner body, bigger database, more media, more vacations, etc.) Ha! I was such a freaked out woman! Instead I collapsed them all into what I reeeeally wanted. Enlightenment. Direct connection with Source. Oneness. Embodiment of Source as my live union. And from that all will unfold for the highest good. YES! Pure yum.

Years ago, this way of living fabulously freaked out my son's father. I told him I was willing to consider a move to wherever he wanted because I trusted his judgment and I knew together we could create the best for our son. I would NEVER have let him win at anything before. I wouldn't have trusted him whatsoever. Now I am filled with faith and trust myself to know what's best, and can empower him to guide us. And while that never ended up happening, we never ended up co-parenting, from afar I can still send him trusting vibes for he and our son to thrive ... and I can stay unattached, trusting, surrendered, and focused on my path to uplift humanity, knowing my son will spend more time with me when it's right.

As I chose to live with what my soul really wanted, I followed my instincts and accepted international speaking engagements and workshops onto my roster, (something that in the past logistically terrified me so I wouldn't even have ventured toward these.) I added more interviews to my schedule, embracing myself as the sensual, spiritual Barbara Walters NOW, traveling locally and internationally to document these conversations on audio and video, not needing to figure out how it was all going to unfold. (Normally that wouldn't work if I didn't have a plan so that I'd feel safe.) More and more media opportunities began effortlessly unfolding. I didn't need them like I used to, in order to feel credible, so that I would seem successful, or so I would be safe! I have softened, with little desire to prepare, simply to come from fullness and serve. Freedom of feminine expression, freedom to speak truths, freedom to be more firm, clear, authentic, and freedom to let my wise oracle rip!

When we're on track in life, I believe we get confirmation or signs to keep unfolding. (And of course the opposite is true isn't it!?)

Years ago a confirmation came in a hand analysis reading, and more recently in a Vedic astrology reading. Ultimately I believe we create our lives and have the power of choice to design our reality. And I also believe there are some predestined circumstances that are meant to support the greatest evolution of our soul this go around. So the hand analysis reader confirmed I am sensitive

-- a gift in that I am empathic, a seer, and a gifted healer, yet conversely I say "Yes" too quickly and too much. Second, the reader said that I am courageous, fiercely loving of my clients, able to sit in the fire and face everything for their freedom, yet conversely will push to the point of exhaustion, serve to the point of sacrifice. Third, the reader told me that I have three unique gifts: I am a clairvoyant, and an oracle, and if I didn't own these capacities they would drain me with stagnation in my life, self-doubt ,and deafen of my intuition. Yikes. What a wake up call again to love myself, own my gifts and serve humanity.

This is true for ALL women!

Adopt healthy boundaries, dissolve the super woman over achiever, see our sensitivities as strengths and trust our intuition.

The second confirmation came in the form of an interview with a gentleman who led ManKind Project workshops for ten years, worked in the highest level of prisons, and has a fascinating explanation of how the Universe works. I discovered that the way I have developed my healing process with clients was extraordinarily similar to his. He too believes that Source is most easily accessed in the body, the pelvis region, free of the spinning mind, with a healed, open heart. Wild. AND while I had to ask many questions for sure, I could actually follow his explanation of how the Universe worked, entertaining insights from spiral dynamics which confirmed that separation, conflict, discomfort, pain ... whatever we call it, is PART of our evolution and that when we resist these energies we compound the blocks. Yet when we embrace the ride, wholeness always returns at a higher ground.

I'm clear that our sensuality is far from fluff. It's our sacred power. Healing doesn't come through our analysis, it happens in the body. Embracing the embodiment of Source through feelings, pictures, intuitions, words -- however it comes for you, and releasing control and softening into the moment, letting beauty nourish your words, your touch, your movements, and your breath ... these practices make you MORE successful, certainly more approachable, inviting, respected, and magnetic.

We can put down our swords and shields.

They are there if we need them.

Yet a shield begets an attack.

Open, wise, discerning hearts magnetize respect, honor, and admiration.

Luminous eyes attract intrigue, affection, attention and magic.

Be the embodiment of Source.

Everything will fall into place from there. I promise.

You CAN have abundance, peace, a thriving relationship, a deep connection with Source, a flourishing family, peace in your body and reverence for life, while you freely express your truth and marvel at the unfolding of miracles that grace your lap.

Face your blindspots.

Stop the running.

End the denial.

Soften into your true power.

Embody Source.

Know you are loved.

Deliciously more now than ever.

CHAPTER 4

THE INVITATION

*"I feel sexy when there's a good base beat and
I feel in tune with dancing with the world."*

- Amy, 26

There is nothing more painful than having a man who totally sees you, celebrates you, wants you and ravishes you and then loses interest in you, checks out other women, withdraws his attention and affection, and even leaves you, alone, crushed and bewildered.

What if I could teach you how to be sexy, feel sexy, and stay sexy so that his affections would not wander but strengthen?

What if I could teach you how to attract a man's devotion forever?

What if I could teach you how to be at peace in every inch of your skin, drinking in mens' appreciation, attention, and celebration of you -- a radiant, luscious, sexy woman?

If you are single, dating, married, divorced, whatever gender identity or sexual orientation, you deserve to be treasured and ravished.

You deserve to feel sensual and luscious.

You're about to learn the recipe to being and staying sexy, and having the love, attention, and adoration you deserve.

Here's the painful truth:

You're either a modern sensual being or you're not. You can't fake it. Men can smell it.

You're either the woman who turns heads when she enters the room or you're not.

You're either the woman men want to ravish and devote their life to or you're not. You're either competitive with other women or you're not.

You're either at peace in every inch of your skin or you're not.

You're either overflowing with passion for life or you're not.

You're either a sensual woman savoring moments with an open heart or you're not.

Moment to moment we either are or are not. Yet the truth is on any given day, we are both. Sometimes we remember and other times we forget. The times we get triggered and forget are painful moments. And that's okay, ;-). It's normal in fact xox

Yet how in the world do we become a sensual woman more often?

What do we let go of? What do we embrace?

How do we get there when we've tried everything?

Well, the first step is to acknowledge how friggin' brilliant you are and if you're brilliance could've told you, it would have by now, right?

So this solution isn't found in your mind. It's not a quick fix, a strategy, an action of doing. It's found in another realm, the realm of non-linear, of energy, of emotions, in the body. Words like intuition, instinct, body intelligence direct us. This is a more subtle realm, a quieter, softer one of patience, deep trust, and respect. A realm of of sacred honor, reverence, the unknown, the mystery.

I'm going to teach you absolutely everything I know, show you all the easy practices that have changed my life and the lives of other women just like you.

You're about to jump off the cliff into the realm of classy seduction, succulence, juiciness, lusciousness, depth, and profound connection to your most feminine core.

There's no way around it but through.

Let's start off big: the truth about why men stop looking at us, why they cheat, why too many women go through this awful experience and how to prevent this from ever happening to you again.

What is the secret to why he doesn't look at me like that anymore?

> We chose a man who never ever had any intention of honoring us, or

> we became too clingy and he needed space, or

> we stopped treating ourselves like a goddess, stopped self-care, stopped nourishing ourselves and thus stopped shining and he saw brighter lights elsewhere.

How do we choose the right man?

Give a man space?

Be the brightest light to keep his affections?

All these answers are found in four components of the practice of "Sensual Self Talk."

1. Body Wisdom

This is how we choose the right man. We use **body wisdom** to form a trusted relationship with our body. It always knows the truth, and we ask it, "How do you feel opening to this man? How do you feel surrendering to this man?" "How do you feel being devoted to this man?" Our heart, our stomach, our solar plexus, our pelvis will either open and feel warm and safe, or it will close, contract and feel tight and restricted. Your job is to listen. And THEN your job is to honor that truth no matter how fat his wallet, no matter how cute he is, no matter what he promises you. Are you ready to trust yourself that much?

2. Self-Affirming Statements

This is how we give a man space. We use **self-affirming statements** to gift a man with his greatest need: freedom. We tell ourselves, "When my man is away, he is challenging himself to be even more deeply on purpose, more able to open me, more able to serve me and the world." "When I give my man space, he adores me and respects me more and showers me with even more attention when he returns."

"When I gift my man with freedom, I cherish the time alone to nourish my body and soul so that when he arrives home I am more luscious than before."

"When I give my good man space, he responds as good men do, with honor, gratitude and devotion."

The bottom line is that to have trust you must give trust. Clinginess repels men. If when he goes out with the guys he betrays your trust and dishonors you, better you find out now and move on. Yet when a good man is gifted with your trust and freedom, he gets the best of both worlds – freedom *and* YOU!

3. Self-Pleasuring Attitude

This is how we remain the brightest lights we can be to attract his affections. We adopt a **self-pleasuring attitude** and know we can only become brighter when WE fill ourselves up.

"I am such a luscious goddess that I will honor myself with healthy eating and exercise today."

"I enjoy my body so much that I take time to caress it with cream every morning."

"I take such pleasure in being a sexual woman that I will walk upon Mother Earth allowing her to fill my pelvis with succulence that I radiate out into the world."

"The more I take care of my sensuality, the more I am showered with attention."

"The more I treasure and give my authentic sexual expression, the more I am met by a great man who honors me."

"I literally turn myself on moment-to-moment as I let existence itself penetrate my body and soul."

A self-pleasuring attitude means taking total responsibility for one's state of sensuality or sexual freedom. Notice the way you talk to yourself when you wait for attention on the outside. It probably feels needy, hopeful, perhaps even desperate. "Please see me. Do you see me? Am I enough?"

Turn this on its head by saying to yourself "I see you. You are more than enough. You are a gorgeous, hot, valuable light." Begin giving a self-pleasuring attitude to yourself immediately and notice that you feel fuller from the inside out. On the outside that acts as magnetism. On the outside it makes you glow and radiate pleasure. On the outside it attracts experiences like men opening doors for you, commenting on how lovely you are, asking you out on dates, suggesting it's time for a weekend away... you've become intoxicating, irresistible and delectable all by insisting to fill yourself up from the inside out first.

Why are most women love-starved, even in their relationship, and what inspires your man's genuine passion and affection in an effortless way? Sexy women are not love-starved because they have learned how to become an invitation to inspire a man's devotion. When we feel absolutely empty, we might look to be filled from the outside in, yet with that approach, I can guarantee you're destined to fail, suffer and become neurotic. We need to learn to be filled from the inside out. You see, being love-starved may *feel* like it's because there's no attention coming from the outside, but it's really a mirror of what's going on inside. And we're all the same. You're not broken or different from anyone else in this respect. I'm the same way and so is Oprah and so is the Dalai Lama. Take heart and begin to do your inner work to give yourself attention and treasure yourself every moment of the day.

If you're feeling love-starved, there's a part of you on the inside that you abandoned, have been avoiding, denying or even making wrong by trying to change it. You may have taken four workshops and read twelve books to try to fix it. Is it working? Probably not. Because by saying "Go away!" you're affirming that something's wrong with a part of you. And that part is getting more angry, more sad or more afraid.

The only answer is allowing that part of you to be, loving it unconditionally and holding it tenderly like you would a child, and telling it that you will hold it for as long as it takes, until the emotion passes. You allow the feelings. You validate the feelings. You be with the feelings. And they will dissolve just as a child's dissolve once they feel heard, understood, and loved for exactly who they are. In fact, it's after the emotion has dissolved that incredible wisdom is revealed, power is taken back and life energy, sexual energy is awakened. More of the how-to on this later.

How truly easy it is to be the one who wins his attention every time, with absolutely no manipulation, withholding or lies. Just pure YOU.

Only a true divine goddess
can win his attention
every time by being exactly
who she is.

The good news is that each of us was born this way. It is our birthright to be her and there is no greater attraction factor for a man than to see us in our authentic, full feminine power radiating for him.

You see, there is a place I go when I dance. I swear that Spirit dances me, some other energy is moving my hips, I feel connected to the earth so much that it's as if I'm making love to the earth with my feet and the energy of openness radiates up through my pelvis. There is a place I go when I breathe deeply that makes my voice lower. My anxiety dissolves and my eyes slightly soften ... like they look after I orgasm ... all lashes. There is a way I look at my son as the light from the sunset streams through his hair that moves me to tears. There is a way that I can sit with my girlfriends on the couch and laugh and cry and we hold each other like sisters and not have to fix a thing and just be open wide to the tragedies and triumphs of life.

This is the place where I go to orgasm by simply dancing. It's like I allow my vagina to soften, I imagine my feet are sucked deep down into moist Mother Earth's realm, I intend that her energy come up into my body and I move my hips in ways that are totally free, past barriers of what people might say, past barriers of what I think is acceptable and proper. I am fully, authentically me dancing with the energy of her. When I start to feel all tingly I allow the energy to build there and don't allow any judgments of myself as bad or nasty. I simply enjoy the pleasure of being a woman on this planet with the capacity to feel pleasure.

Sometimes I cry and release shame, sometimes I ride waves of soft ripple like an orgasm and moan, and sometimes I even gush. They are not clitoral, intense orgasms you can get riding a snowmobile (I'm Canadian). They are g-spot, wavy orgasms that go on and on. Over time through practice (I've been taking dance movement classes for years and dancing on my own as well), I can orgasm just looking at a man, kissing him, sucking him, without him ever touching me. It's like I'm willing to turn myself on. I'm willing to enjoy being a woman. I'm willing to enjoy pleasure with no shame. Nothing in my life has felt more freeing than being totally at peace with my body and it's enjoyment of pleasure. The more you practice letting go, the more this energy will take you to ecstasy, too.

Now, back to getting a man's attention. A woman who lives in her body, in her hips, is open to the energy moving through her pelvis. This woman wins a man's attention every time. Think about it symbolically: he's a penis wanting to enter a vagina. What is it about your "vagina-ness" that draws him, pulls him, from a deep place in his heart? What makes him want to penetrate you with his phallus yet also penetrate you with his heart, his mind, his soul?

Many women are superficially sexy and yes, that can win his penis's attention but then he'll wander. A woman who can let go of trying to control the situation and simply savor moments through her breath, her body, her vagina, and her heart becomes such a juicy invitation that she becomes one of the women men die for.

And this does NOT mean you're a tramp or sleazy or easy. You are at choice of who you will open to and when. Yet you can always open in trust to the Universe, 24/7 you can flirt with the breeze. Every moment on a date you can savor smells, sights, sounds, tastes, words, and touch. There is never a reason to disconnect from pleasure for YOU. This fills you to the brim, eliminates neediness, turns him on to see you as beauty itself, and then you get to decide what you'd like to invite him to do next. You get to feel into his nobility and whether you'll let him lead.

Yet if you're all tensed up, in control, in your head, you don't have the capacity to even know the depth of this man, and that's when we make bad decisions and get hurt. Your power is in your hands ... open and soften to you.

4. Openness -- Embracing All that Is

When a woman is **fully open,** filled to the brim and overflowing, alive, passionate, feeling dynamic and soooo at peace with who she is and where she is in life ... all that springs forth through her is divine ... it looks like gratitude for life, it looks like collaboration with other women, it looks like cooperation with her partner and family, it looks like a wet pussy when she makes love, it looks like confidence as she dresses, and radiance when she walks into a room.

When a woman shuts down, closes off, constricts, contracts, withholds the truth, says yes when she means no, doesn't put herself first and begins to operate on fumes, panicked, in scarcity, barely keeping it together ... she feels this way because she has not only clamped down and cut off the flow of the Universe through her, she's spinning in her head trying to be in control on her own, not aware she can BE a vessel through which the Universe can flow, so she can concrete with the All. My orgasms became multiple and also ejaculatory when I began to understand I was the vessel through which life poured. It's called surrender -- yet this kind of surrender is not about giving in or giving up -- it's about giving over to an energy that's holding you if you'll let it ... it's about having the courage to jump off a cliff and in faith let go, resting in the arms of THE Mother herself.

Being open is not for the weak of heart.

It is for the bold, the courageous, the Amazon warrior, the high priestess in you. And it is a choice moment to moment. You never get there; you simply get to open and open again and again with everything life brings you.

AND being open is also preparing yourself to be more open. It grows and grows and you get stronger and stronger.

Each moment you decide ...

- Do I want to say yes to this request?

- Did I rest and rejuvenate my body?

- Did I clear my mind?

- Did I spend time in gratitude?

- Did I commune with Mother Nature?

- Did I let go of resentments?

- Did I look with love at myself naked in the mirror this morning?

- Did I honor my yearnings and masturbate or initiate making love with my partner?

- Did I stuff my feelings and put on a happy face?

- Did I make time to feel my feelings, have a good cry, punch a pillow, be heard by my best friend, create a sacred time to talk with my lover, snuggle profoundly with my beloved before drifting to sleep?

Here is some very honest feedback I've received from some of you over the years that I'm including in the hope that it will help you magnetize a magnificent man, and I've offered my responses and some expansion on the ideas presented in the comments.

"Being sexy, flirty, soft seems so weak. I've worked hard for my success and want to be valued for my accomplishments and my beauty."

When I lived in LA, I used to regularly attend Agape and Marianne Williamson's Monday nights before she ran for the presidency. We speak similarly in validating every step of evolution. I believe we have had to and still must expand our masculine energy and stand up for our right to vote, equal pay, protect ourselves from rape, protect our sisters from sexual slavery, trafficking, and genital mutilation. And yet in so doing we have mistakenly devalued our softness, our receptivity, disconnecting from one another as sisters, destroying our collaborative and cooperative capacities to solve problems, feeling superior if we don't ask for help, feeling sorry for women who don't work, feeling like a failure if we aren't perfect, being unwilling to receive support because doing it alone looks good.

It's time to swing back into balance. Clearly we're unwilling to manipulate with our sexuality knowing it turns us symbolically into a piece of meat. Yet Source, Spirit, Intelligence, God, and creativity itself is a flow of energy that inflates, ignites and awakens us through our body, animating us into divine action, illuminating our divine minds, radiating a power that bonds families and heals relationships. And let's remember, it takes more courage to surrender, soften, open and allow, rather than to stay hardened and in control.

The comment above about being "sexy, flirty" could very well be an act, a put-on. What movies make you think you need to be something like that in order to score the guy? Flirt with an agenda and it's a manipulation. Yet how about flirting with life, the breeze, the plants, the water, the sunset! It's you saying YES to life, letting yourself be moved by beauty. And that's a gift that mesmerizes a quality man.

And finally, having coached hundreds of men personally, I have seen clearly that men respect us for our accomplishments, however I've also learned that's not why he'll marry you. He marries you because your heart is open, you inspire his purpose, and your radiance intoxicates him. He marries you for the warmth of your body and touch, for your praise of his purpose, for your acknowledgement that he makes a difference in your life.

"You talk so fluffy like a floozie. Great for masculine attention yet I highly doubt men respect you, because I don't respect you. Yet I hate to admit you're right. I'm frustrated that men tell me I intimidate them. I don't know where to turn."

I had to deep breathe through this one yet she knows I make mistakes too. I've been scared, frustrated, and insecure, and said cruel things or sent condescending looks at a sister. I don't adore the way she addressed me, but I get it, I'll forgive her. And I forgive me for the times I betrayed a sister.

Now to listen more deeply to her statement.

She was willing to call one on herself. We can hear her crunchiness, her anger, her depleted state of hopelessness, and even her loneliness.

She's made a similar mistake to the above comment seeing my sensuality as fluffy. Now as I wrote earlier, I have undergone yet another transformation in my authentic feminine expression so on one level, I'll agree. There have been times when I may have been over the top to try to make a point, in my earlier days of embracing my expertise, in trying to be enough, in trying to make a difference, in trying to be accepted.

And yet she's taken the opposite and arguably even more devastating route of being intimidating. While we are all ever-evolving beings, my courage to be open, to explore, to make mistakes, to pick myself up, to do my work to heal my heart, to release the past, to forgive men and myself, to brave letting go and being vulnerable ... all of these practices have led me to the most empowered, expansive, confident, sensual, feminine experience of my life.

I remember when Dr. Northrup told me to just wait 'til I was 50! Well, I'm 50, and she's right! It IS even better than I could ever imagine … I'm looking forward to 60 and beyond, xox.

Choosing the way of intimidating men is easier. Safer. Righteous. Separating. And also, lonely. There is a fulfillment in accomplishment, in money, in meeting goals, and I respect that. Yet not at the demise of one's softness, suppleness, openness, for this turns us into men and we attract wimpy guys who we can boss around. Yuck.

For this sister, I would first invite her to tell the truth. She's using intimidation because she's mad at men. To which I suggest, honor that and heal that. Then tell the truth that she's using intimidation because she's scared to let go of control. Then, honor that and heal that. Then tell the truth with everything else she finds. Does she believe she's enough? Does she trust God? Does she need to learn to fall in love with herself, accomplishments aside, just pure her? Her journey will be intense, yet like pressure on coal, she will emerge as a diamond as so many of my clients have … balanced in their feminine and masculine energies, feeling THEIR truth in femininity, authentic in their expression, feeling softer, safer, more sultry, classy, open and alive. And only from HERE can her ideal partner even see her, let alone claim her to her core.

CHAPTER 5

TURNING THE TABLES

*"I feel sexy when I'm connected to my inner flow, inner knowing,
inner core, when I'm allowing myself to be taken care of,
to be loved and supported."*

- Tarnie, 49

Just an aside … before you keep embracing more secrets about how men's and women's relationships work around sexuality and sensuality … I wanted to let you know that each chapter begins with a quote from an every day real woman like you. They are women I know from dance class, the chiropractor's office, my Goddess Group, and my local pizzeria, all generously sharing their insights for us to savor. We are all connected, all One.

Here's another point of view I've gathered from clients:

*"The horrifying truth that once a man has "claimed" you,
he subtly sabotages your sexiness— how do I turn the tables,
keep my sexiness and keep him wanting me?"*

Think about it, Gorgeous one … he's caught the fairest one of all!!! The rarest gem! The most exquisite queen! He starts to plot. "There's no way in Hell any other guy is going to get a chance to swipe her away from me. So I'll take her out and show her off, yet dog-gonnit, when she's out on the town without me, she'd better not shine too brightly. I sure don't want her to get any more powerful guy's attention or I'll be out of luck."

I don't even think guys do this consciously. They simply discourage you to wear hot clothes when going out with the girls. They don't mention it if you put on a little weight just to be sure you can't go run off and attract another guy. They don't mind if your career is not too successful so that you won't be out there meeting lots of people because they want to be sure they can keep their "prey."

The unfortunate thing is that if we buy into this, WE start to lose his interest! What he thought would keep us is now making him less attracted to us! Not good. So the way to turn the tables is to keep shining, keep being sexy, keep attracting the attention of men, keep being the seductive, sensual, succulent goddess you are AND keep him coming after you. Don't rub it in his face or play games, just invite him to meet you out at a bar and let him see that other men are interested in you and then when he arrives, say something in a way that he can hear, "Excuse me, it was great talking to you but my MAN is here."

Let a girls' night out, where he's afraid other men will be the recipient of your sensual expression, be the night where you come home the naughtiest, the horniest, and the most fired up to attack him, and he will soon start to understand that when you fill yourself up with girl time, he gets the benefits in the end.

And finally remember that you're not being sexy for him. On some level you're doing it as a gift to him, yet ultimately you're being sexy for YOU! For the joy of it, the pleasure of it, for the sake of being alive on this planet as a juicy woman. It's your birthright to experience your full sexual expression. This shift may dissolve any of the above silliness when he comes to understand on some level that he simply lives with sexuality herself.

I HAVE seen a woman who totally embraced this. She dressed up for a night out with her friends as much as she did with her husband. When she returned from her girl's night, she was so vibrant, alive, juicy, and grateful for him watching the kids, that she attacked him for a night of profound passion. Then he began asking HER when was she going out with so and so again! AND he even figured out which friends she'd been out with when she came home being the most sensual. He could see who balanced her out.

Here is a three-second practice that will show you how to transform feelings of insecurity and unworthiness into feelings of unshakeable confidence and radiant lusciousness.

- Breathe deeply.

- Relax your shoulders.

- Open your heart.

- Relax your stomach.

- Keep breathing as you soften your pelvis.

- Imagine opening your vagina lips.

- Imagine literally straddling the Earth.

- Imagine breathing up Mother Earth's energy into your vagina.

- Breathe her into your soft belly, your solar plexus power center.

- Imagine you ARE the Earth.

- You ARE as wide and lush as a forest.

- You ARE as deep and vast as the ocean.

- You ARE as fierce and bold as a tornado.

- You ARE as tender and sweet as the breeze rippling over a wheat field at sunset.

- Keep breathing.

How do you feel? Yummier?

Next, there are three magnetic tools that make a man want to ravish you sexually AND stay devoted to you for life … I call them **The Art of Sexual Invitation**

When we're trying to turn men on, they might be attracted to us but they won't be devoted to us past the morning after, because on some level they know we are needy and trying to make them think we're good enough, sexy enough, worthy enough of being made love to. It's this energy where we feel used in the morning. Unconscious men prey on women like this. So what do we do? We DON'T try to turn them on. Yet even when we're NOT trying to turn them on, men might still be attracted to us. But they won't be devoted past tomorrow. This is because our attention is on ourselves: "I can open my own door thank you very much. I have my own vibrator and don't need you, thank you very much." You see, energetically, we're not open because in the past they've probably hurt us, betrayed us, let us down. On the one hand this is a step in the right direction away from needy to confident.

Notice that it's the other side of the same coin, going from overly wanting him to overly not wanting him. It's a reaction to his past behavior, not a powerful choice of yours in the moment, to being open, to deserving and attracting a good man. Yes, your protection mechanism is valid for sure as mens' actions can truly damage our sense of self, and yet be assured that only an open woman who is practicing the Art of Sexual Invitation can attract a good man who is worthy and capable of cherishing her.

The only way to both attract a man and keep him devoted to you forever is to cultivate three things: pleasure in your body, pleasure opening your heart, and pleasure fiercely loving a man.

1. Pleasure in Your Body

The key here is to have pleasure being a woman. Have pleasure being in the body you have right now, not the one you want. Have pleasure in the way your hips feel in your jeans, how your breasts feel in your bra, how it feels to walk along the sidewalk and feel the Earth pushing back up against you, how it feels to have the breeze move your hair, how it literally feels to have existence itself press up against your every inch and meet you the way you like to be met. When THIS is where your focus is, your consciousness is, you are irresistible because he wants to experience the pleasure you are feeling inside when he's inside you.

2. Pleasure Opening Your Heart

Men want to know that even if you get pissy, you'll keep your heart open and not kill him off (shut down his spirit with your words, your eyes, and your thoughts). He wants to know that you can be afraid of what's happening in the economy or with his job yet you're not going to shut down and leave — you'll keep your heart open and stay the course with him. He wants to know that you will not become a bitter old hag, or angry at the world. Instead, you'll be able to forgive life's hardships and keep your heart open, shining, and optimistic. He wants to know that no matter if you have a fight or even feel totally insecure as a new mom or in a new job, you won't push him away -- you can feel your fear and still keep your heart open to him for him to ravish you, and love you in your juicy and luscious openness. He wants to know that your open-hearted devotion to him is unwavering. This will make him devoted to you -- and only you -- forever.

3. Pleasure Fiercely Loving a Man

Your man wants to know that you're not a pushover. He wants to know that you'll stand by him because you stand up to him. He wants to feel that you believe in him so much that you won't put up with him selling out on his purpose. He wants to know you can hold him to the fire, insisting he live fully, give his gifts fully, and never give up, no matter what. There is fierceness to a woman who is willing to be angry from love. No man would be crazy enough to be devoted to a nagging bitch, yet watch how he stands stand up taller when you unleash your loving fury on him: "I f*&%'ing love you and it kills me to see you not living your dreams!" It's like the ocean when the storm is crashing. You are the ocean, sometimes calm and sometimes fierce. You've got to cultivate the ability to be strong, hold a man to his purpose with love and let him know that he'll never be able to look you in the eyes as anything less than his most noble presence. He has to know you believe in him when all else fails and that YOU are the fire he'll have to deal with if he ever gives up on his dream. Now THAT is a woman men die for.

Another common question I receive stems from being hurt, used, and betrayed and women have every right to be skeptical, gun shy, or closed off. However, that keeps us alone, thus let's explore how to spot a less than noble man and say goodbye before he breaks your heart.

For the mind:

Does he call you to claim you? Is he on time? Is he looking at other women? Is he all pompous, identifying himself with his "things" instead of with the substance of his purpose? Does he remember things you've told him? Is he too good to be true and not real, not authentic, not human, an answer to your little girl but not your powerful queen? Is he coming on too strong and not treating you like a goddess?

For the heart:

Even though he may come through in spades with the above, the main question is this: Is he present with you? I mean impeccably. I mean is he so "with" you that you can surrender, relax, trust, and be you? You can if he is present with you more in your mind than in your body. Is your body opening? Does your heart feel safe? Does your pelvis feel soft and yearning? Does your power center at the solar plexus feel competitive or honored?

- You will FEEL if he is noble more then you will KNOW if he's noble.

- Slow down enough to really listen to the messages in your body.

- Ask your friends if you appear "queenly" or "little girl" when you talk about him.

- Always, and I mean always, trust your body.

Next, here is another question that had come straight from your emails to me:

"Letting a man see me sweat scares me.
I know I only show him my perfect side yet I'm scared
to be taken advantage of and hate feeling vulnerable."

This question reminds me of taking a live caller's question after an interview in my Intimate Conversations series. This is the human condition. Men don't want to show you their fears either. Yet think about this logically. You show up inauthentically, saying something like, "No, I'm fine really." Then he shows up inauthentically and says something like, "No, I'm cool, really." You end up with two inauthentic liars aching to be seen, heard, valued, and unconditionally loved for who they are.

The question comes down to this. Who's going to go first?

I like short cuts so I say – you! You go first. And this means addressing the little girl inside you. She is scared. Listen to her. The back and forth dialogue with her goes like this:

>You: "So, you're scared if we tell him the truth that he'll hurt us, huh?"
>
>Little Girl: "Yeah... he'll hurt us bad."
>
>You: "So, you're saying if we show him our fears he'll hurt us, will he?"
>
>Little Girl: "Well yeah ... or at least he'll make fun of us."
>
>You: "So you're saying he'll make fun of us if he sees our fears, is that right?"
>
>Little Girl: "Yeah, and that will hurt my feelings if he makes fun of me."
>
>You: "Right, your feelings will be hurt if he makes fun of you."
>
>Little Girl: "Well, I guess I don't care if he makes fun of me. I just really want him to like me.
>
>You: "Ahhh, you really want him to like you, yes."
>
>Little Girl: "Yeah, I really like him."
>
>You: "Got it, he's really special to you."
>
>Little Girl: "Yeah, he's special, so maybe let's just be ourself and let him know we like him."
>
>You: "Cool, so you want us to just be ourself and let him know we like him?"
>
>Little Girl: "Yeah ... we'll be okay no matter what. We're cool."
>
>You: "Yeah... we're cool all right. Thanks for reminding me of that."
>
>Little Girl: "You're welcome."

Isn't that amazing? When we don't resist ... the internal conversation can shift to positive in an embodied, natural, real, and solid way. Yet when we resist and tell the Little Girl inside to shut up ... she generally sabotages us. Notice that what started out as fear has turned into peace. Being vulnerable with ourselves allows us to be vulnerable with another. Just excuse yourself to the restroom, go through this conversation, and see how the rest of the night goes.

Here's another question from a sister:

"Letting go of my goals, letting go of control, letting go and doing these sensual practices you speak of seems stupid, yet when I began to try them, they actually made me feel panicked. I don't want to let go of control and be open to abuse."

Yes. When we've only known life swimming upstream, turning around and going with the flow of the river will seem stupid at first. And then yes, it can be very scary. What I can tell you from being on the other side is that it's almost like a belief system has to die and be reborn, an identity is shattered, a total reality is destroyed. When I let go, as I shared in the early pages of the book, I thought I was having a nervous breakdown. I couldn't stop crying. That wasn't cool. Not fun. No way.

Yet because I was unwilling to live a life of permanent struggle, suffering, pushing, stress, fear and disconnection, I was willing to see what was on the other side. I mean could it really be worse?

What I found on the other side was the flow, which is the present moment. You may not have gripping control, yet you do have choice. In the world of panicked control you had to keep your sword and shield up 24/7. In the present moment, in openness, you are connected to ALL THAT IS, every bit of brilliance, guidance, support, protection, ideas, creativity, power, strength, and ingenuity possible. AND you don't have to try. It's just all there. That's why it's written that your power is found in the present moment.

When you let your edges soften and stop having to have it all figured out, limitless ideas grace the landscape of your mind, endless waves of quiet fulfillment fill your cells, and sultry embers burn to ignite your heart. Radiance itself showers from your eyes. That's all pretty poetic. So down and dirty this means that in a conversation you don't have to worry about what to say, it will flow organically. When you meet someone you're approachable and there's space, room and the capacity for him to ask for your number. This means that you'll walk into a room at peace with you, your day, gently eager to delight in the yet-unrevealed serendipitous events of the evening.

This means you exhale before needing an external reason to exhale. This feels like effortless confidence, this looks like -- Who Is That Woman?

And one last thing, about abuse ... in the flow, the present moment, in openness ... you have access to the highest response in each moment, the capacity to protect yourself should you need to, the awareness of your intuition which is an instinct on what feels right and what doesn't ... capacities you don't have access to when shut down, closed off and afraid. Your self-trust will sky rocket and proof that you can take care of yourself will soften you even more.

And of course, I'm sure you're clear that you will be hurt again, right?

Life equals night and day, up and down, left and right, pain and pleasure, hurt and bliss. It's an experience. People are not perfect. We are real. We make mistakes. We make amends. We grow, evolve and commit to being a field of love as Marianne Williamson told us my group one night, because we can, and because we need to, to turn this Titantic around.

I am stronger in my vulnerability than I ever was in my closure. You can hold more sand in a softly cupped hand. Jujitsu black belts are soft, flexible and loose in their moment of greatest fear on the mat. Yes, this is masterful living I'm teaching. And you can do it. You're ready.

CHAPTER 6

ART OF ALLURING

"I feel sexy when I fit in my 'skinny jeans,' when I go to the gym and feel good about myself and eat healthy."

- Titina, 33

It's important to me that you know what makes men disrespect you, dishonor you, use you, and place you in a category of short term entertainment versus long term potential. My intention is to save you heartache and bring you happiness.

The three biggest mistakes women make trying to be sexy that actually turn men off:

- Being too provocative with dress, makeup, willingness to have sex quickly -- says insecurity (with a red flag).

- Being too clingy physically and not granting them freedom to claim YOU -- screams needy.

- Being too sultry, rehearsed, porn star-like, ridiculously moaning -- all says inauthentic -- they'll do you for their satisfaction and be done with you.

So the opposite sounds like this:

- Dress classy, feminine, authentic in a way that makes you feel alive and luscious.

- Physically attend to your man yet remember more that you are a piece of art to admire, to claim, and to ravish, so make your body into an invitation -- be willing to drop your hankie!

- Let go of what you think sexy is and just be you — sink into your body, breathe deeply, savor moments, express your true feelings, feel your devotion for who he is in the world, have pleasure in your body as you sit, eat, walk, talk, make love. There's nothing like the real thing!!!

The three sultry secrets to having his lasting attention, touch, and affection for you for the rest of your life ... you deserve this!

Now this one may take you aback because it's counterintuitive. Normally, when we want something we go out and get it, right? That is masculine energy: directed, purposeful, go get 'er done!! Feminine energy is receiving, allowing, inviting, and receptive, and has the capacity to wait for eternity, only to be delighted to have everything laid at our feet.

So the **Three Secrets to Keep Him Coming Back** for more require you to let go of him and give to YOU!

ENCOURAGE HIM TO HAVE GUY TIME

If you're glad to have him out of your hair and enjoy a night to yourself, great!! Be sure to fill yourself up in ways that nourish your spirit from the inside out. If you're not feeling so great about encouraging him to go out, feel any feelings of abandonment, rejection, loneliness or not enough when he leaves. Don't blame these feelings on him. This is your own personal quiet time to reflect on why your heart is closing. It's time to feel the feelings you have been repressing. Let them surface with compassion for yourself, breathe into them, let them dissolve and see what wise lesson graces your consciousness. You may need to validate and unconditionally love a part of yourself that was rejected in the past. You may need to forgive someone who hurt you due to their unconsciousness. You have the power to set yourself free if you validate and love the "dark" parts of yourself. Fill the void of time away from him with self-love, self-care, and pleasure from the inside out. Intend to feel the pleasure of simply being a sensual woman. Slowly begin to enjoy your own company and allow the old neediness to transform into healthy heartfelt gratitude for connection with your beloved. Let this flood your open heart and notice the difference when he sees you when he gets home. You will radiate fullness, confidence, self-worth, and acceptance. What a magical place for him to enter into your home and into your body.

YOU TAKE NOURISHING GIRL TIME

Nothing in this world can replace a great group of women -- women that hear you, see you, love you, and will tell you the truth. Let go of any time spent with women who gossip, man bash, compete, or complain. Life is too short to spend your precious downtime with people who bring you down. Check in after a phone call, a cup of coffee, a quick trip to the mall, or a full on girl's night out. Are you depleted or nourished? Did you feel heard? Did you relax to your core and not have to work to get a word in? Did you feel reminded of your worth for being exactly who you are?

Spend regular time with goddesses who remind you of your worth and celebrate a sensual existence. Be willing to bring up to the group that you want to begin the night by telling each other, one by one, fully and completely, what's sexy about her. We say we'd get embarrassed yet honestly it's what we crave. We're starving to be seen, appreciated and acknowledged. Once you've filled each other up, notice that men around the place start noticing you! You'll all be buzzing with sensual energy, open and alive, like a flower in bloom — and the bees will come! Promise!

AND … if you're on your way home to your man after this nourishing delicious girl's night out, you'll be luscious and yummy and ready to attack him and he won't know what hit him but he'll be grateful and most likely encourage you to go out with these women again!

Note: remember the opposite is true also. Your man might be perfectly kind that day yet after a night out with women who man bash or complain, you'll come home finding something wrong with him, you won't get the attention you desire and he'll give you a hard time next time you want to go out with your friends. You have all the power so choose wisely.

THE MODERN WAY TO DANCE FOR HIM

I remember when I surprised my first husband with a sexy little dance while he was working from home and he shooed me away saying he was "too busy". Ouch. The second husband got all nervous and fidgety when I would strip for him. Argh!!! But who's the only one in common here?

Me.

Point taken.

So, I signed up for pole dancing class and was in tears by the second session. I could open and express myself in a small box yet any sexual and sensual expression outside of that comfort zone made me terrified, feel ashamed, afraid of being rejected, and afraid to be judged. I learned that I was attracting men who were uncomfortable with their sexuality just like me! So I moved through it and WOW! My last long-term boyfriend LOVED me dancing for him and what was great was that I actually enjoyed it, too! I learned to love my body, my expression, my coyness, my inner nasty girl as well as my goddess, my queen, my sacred feminine spirit.

GO FOR IT!

Dance for him.

Dance all the parts of you, all the flavors and varieties of you!

FIRST dance for yourself and come to peace with exactly who you are. Perfectly imperfect. Whole and complete. Glorious, luscious you.

Next lets learn about **Long Term Turn-On!**

Inside strategies from successfully married women on how to not only keep but build sexual chemistry year after year.

Let's think about this. If chemistry between us and our partner is to be sustained or even build year to year, it would make logical sense that something within us has to be sustained or built year to year, right?

How about building our self-esteem, our self-worth, our self-value, our sensual expression, our sexual freedom, our openness to all that is, and our willingness to say YES to life?

The best way I know to do this is NOT in my head, but in my body: dancing.

DANCE – YOUR BODY IS YOUR KEY TO FREEDOM

Sounds simple enough and it can be done simply enough. But I mean *really* dance. Dance to turn YOUR self on. We can more easily dance to turn on our partners, but what if you danced in the mirror and enjoyed your own temptress? How comfortable are you with your body? Could you light candles and turn the lights low and dance naked, feeling any shame that arose and keep dancing anyways? Could you stand naked in front of the mirror and send love to the areas of your body you normally send punishment to? Could you watch yourself in the mirror and give pleasure to yourself without shame, basking in the miracle of your body's ability to experience bliss? Could you sign up for a pole dancing class and explore the edges of where you judge your sexuality and sensuality? Could you have an erotic toy and lingerie party at your home for you and your friends and really stretch your edge?

The point isn't to do all these things just to do them.

The point is to embrace each suggestion as a way to expand your self-love and peace with your authentic sensual and sexual nature. The point is to face, love, and release any shame you have about yourself and let your true light shine. Sexiness isn't so much the lace panties and eyeliner as is it a woman who knows she's sexy exactly as she is.

Could you be so at peace in your skin, so at peace with your body, so at peace with your expression and savoring moments that you fully opened to each moment, breathed in each moment, exhaled YOU into the moment, the gift of you into the moment, and then shut the door behind you never to look back, only to open yourself up again to the next moment?

Could you do this during a dinner date, during love-making? It is this kind of trust, surrender, embracing of life that makes a sexy woman. She knows that she can bring her best to each moment, even if her best some days is to hide. She loves herself even when she's scared and she has the courage to breathe in another breath again and open to the unknown.

This kind of openness and courage makes for completely ravishing, deeply profound, deliciously dark, mind-blowing sex. I really want you to get that YOU are the catalyst for being sexy, staying sexy and having the best sex of your life.

I dance for myself, for my lover, with women at pole dancing classes, with men and women at movement classes, and there is always a place I bump up against where I want to stop, pull back, do it right, look good, be safe, hide. And it's my intention to love myself more and more each day, to release all the shame that has bound me, to be so out of my head and in my body that I am totally open and savoring life moment to moment. I have been told there is nothing sexier than a woman who loves to be in her body and I know there's nothing that makes me happier, regardless of the outside's opinion, than to be at peace with who I am.

BE gentle with yourself as the feelings come up.

There have been weeks at a time when I wouldn't stop welling up with tears as I danced as some pain was being released. Trust the process. Your body knows what it's doing. Let spirit have its way with you. Turn over your pain, fears and concerns to the energy that's dancing your body. Learn to love all your shades of emotions. And KNOW, and I can promise you on this one, that the sadness, anger, shame or fear will pass and you will settle into the true depth of who you are -- a sensual woman.

The mind-blowing secret that almost no woman knows about that makes him chase after you even after you're dating or married: You have to be able to get him out of a bad mood.

Whenever a man is in a bad mood, he's in his head. He's trying to figure out how he can make something happen, change something, fix something, achieve something and kill something! He's trying to figure this out from his head which is a file folder of the past strategies of achievement and failure. Your job is to get him out of his head and into his body. Why? Because that's where intuition lies, where the power of spirit comes through, where answers to problems lie. You see, both men and women have masculine and feminine energy inside them. In general, men have more masculine energy and women have more feminine energy. His strategies will work much better when the solution is sourced from his body in the feminine energy, just as the same is true for you.

Sooooo the way to get him there is through YOUR body.

Don't try this when he's pacing on the phone or really irritated such that he'd verbally abuse you. Just FEEL into the right moment to come from total service, total unconditional loving for this pained soul, like a divine concubine whose job it is to love this man until he understands his power, until he lets go of his mind and enters his body's wisdom through connecting with your body.

You may do this through pushing him down on the couch and giving him a blow job. You may do this by making him sit down and giving him a strip tease. No words, just actions. Penetrate his gaze with your deep love and devotion to him past his mood to his bold purpose in life. The point is not to ask for anything in return verbally or energetically, not to make him feel like he needs to do anything other than receive your body's touch. He needs resuscitation, he needs a life line, he's almost dead in the juices of creativity and you are his savior.

Give this gift of your body as a way for him to regain sanity. When he comes to he will be so grateful, he will have regained his connection to Source energy and either have a solution to his problem or at least feel like he can handle it. Whether in that moment or later once he's handled the issue that bothered him in the first place, he will see you as his lady, his woman, his goddess, his high priestess, and his divine concubine. When a man has been so erotically and lovingly served by the feminine, nothing will ever break that bond. You are his forever.

CHAPTER 7

WHAT TURNS ME OFF

"I feel sexy when I'm singing
and the divine feminine is singing through me,
when I'm in grubby clothes and rollerblading and totally free."

- Silvie, 30

I can't go any further in suggesting what to do without telling you what not to do. In fact, it's not really about "doing" at all. These next ten practices are the secret behind why all my tips and tools work. It's kind of like in that movie Karate Kid where he had to do "wax on, wax off" and paint the whole fence before he was ready for Karate. These "being" practices will help you effortless and easily BE a sexy woman who attracts all the love, affection and attention you deserve.

10 THINGS TO STOP DOING
SO YOU CAN BE A JUICY, SEXY WOMAN

1. **Stop thinking from your head** and think from your body, your heart, your pelvis, as if your pelvis is your brain, your

intelligence, your wisdom. Trust feelings more than words. Notice that if you breathe into your pelvis and trust that gut "uh-huh" or "uh-uh" that your man will be way more receptive than when you run at the mouth. (Yes, I know how right you are, how eloquent you are, but you're pushing him away, so stop!) Respond to him with a sound that shows your hurt, your pain or your pleasure and bliss. Notice that your feelings are always trying to tell you something to help honor your self-worth, guard you from those who don't value you, show you where you could expand or forgive. Sometimes there's nothing better than a good cry session to reveal the truth in your heart.

2. **Stop worrying about how you stack up to the next woman.** Instead come from overflowing abundance which allows you to see a sister in every woman you meet. Ask yourself the questions. What do I believe about myself that I insist on sizing myself up against other women? The answer for me wasn't pretty. I was afraid I wasn't as attractive or sexy and she'd get my man, get more attention, and get the promotion rather than me. I realized that it wasn't her but ME who had the work to do with my self-esteem, and I began to ask the question ... What is it that I celebrate in my sisters? How can I savor the fact that there's plenty for everyone? The truth is that you'll find the answer if you ask. Choose to be full of faith and trust your innate worth. Notice the support that showers your life when you're willing to rest into feminine energy and enjoy collaboration, cooperation, support and celebration.

3. **Stop holding your stomach and vagina tight, thinking this will somehow keep you safe.** Instead, let go of control by letting go physically and feel the energy, the serendipity flow around you. For years, perhaps decades, I walked around with a tight stomach and clenched vagina. It was as if I was bracing for a hit, protecting myself before the strike, on guard before

anyone even said anything. I was TERRIFIED to let go and felt absolutely vulnerable to being taken advantage of. The unfortunate result of this was terrible digestion problems, adrenal exhaustion and energetically, I was unconsciously pushing away everyone and everything that I so desperately wanted. You see, I wanted it, yet I was physically preparing myself for the blow of not getting it, thus it never came. Begin by being conscious of where you hold your tension in your body. Begin to notice the "why" underneath it. What story are you telling yourself that might have been true when you were five years old, but is no longer true, and is now holding away the very love, attention and affection you desire? Begin to relax these areas and breathe into them when driving, when at work, when on a date, when making love. Begin to sink into the Earth when you walk, begin to breathe deeper and feel what comes up. You may need to dance at home at night and make space for yourself to cry. I had to release quite a few tears until I could find the trust to let go and open. AND YET WHEN I FINALLY DID, that's when the hugest rush of love and feminine energy came flowing into my body. Orgasms were off the charts. Creativity was flowing. Attention from men in every situation. More clients. More fun with my son. More peace being me.

4. **Stop being dramatic and having addictive intellectual stories about your emotions and processes.** Instead start feeling in your body, expressing more sounds and fewer words to communicate your truth. I was the queen of drama. I was a damn good story teller and I could convince any of you to validate my victim story. I would get all fired up, cry hysterically, exhaust myself and get attention. Yet how was it working for me? Did the crying actually help? No. Did the attention I got make me feel any better? No. So what was the problem? Shutting in emotions wasn't the answer because

they eventually boiled up and I would kill someone off with an outburst.

The answer was that I was being dramatic and crying in order to get attention, rather than to heal and move on. I felt that if I let go of my story, I would be all alone. What I learned was that when I cried without self-judgment, no victim/poor me at all, simply cried as if releasing bottled up energy, I felt more at peace. I was holding the space for me to cry like the Universe was holding me and loving me unconditionally and I would simply feel without trying to change how I felt or get rid of the feeling, as if the Universe was willing to hold me for days, weeks, years if needed. Then miraculously the sorrow (or anger or fear) passed and I was free. In fact MORE people gave me attention, but now in a good way. They weren't people who only liked me because I was a victim and would validate their sorry story as well. No, they were positive people, optimistic and conscious people. And then began the stream of noble men who were all of a sudden attracted to me, a sexy woman at peace with her heart. Hmmm...

5. **Stop trying to control the world by being nice and getting people to like you by manipulating them or allowing them to manipulate you.** Start simply breathing fully in and out and being with people in the moment, authentically curious about what might happen next. Even though we'd all like to believe we can control life, control people, control outcomes, I know you know we can't. Yes, we can try and that's exhausting and futile, disappointing and infuriating. What if you gave up right now in this moment the behavior of controlling situations to get attention, controlling situations to be the sexiest you think you could be? What if you stopped trying to get people to like you, to approve of you, to give you affection or attention? I know MY EGO is screaming, "Okay, sure. And be alone the rest of my life?" Yes, our dear ego would like us to believe that, which is why most of us are

NOT getting the attention and adoration we deserve! When you stop trying to GET (from the outside) and start giving yourself (from the inside) attention, adoration, affection, love, sensual affirmation, permission to sexually express your truth and NOT wait for another to give it to you, you take back your power. You literally plug yourself into a huge surge of power.

Start treasuring yourself with your actions, your thoughts, your behaviors. As ridiculous as it sounds, talk to yourself in the mirror (or in your head if you're at work!) and tell yourself how hot you are, how incredible you are, how much you are a gift to this world. Now the ego will pipe up and say, "Well then you'll become arrogant". Thank your ego for sharing, but that's BS. I've never met a client in my private practice that has come in complaining of getting too much love growing up. What happens when we start to give ourselves the attention we crave? We start to have the experience mirrored back to us in the world. Just like when you believe you're sexy, so do men. You literally let go of trying to DO something to GET a result from the outside world and begin giving yourself attention on the inside and all of a sudden people ask if you've had a face lift, are you in love, did you lose ten pounds? Self-love looks good on you. It's inviting, sexy and seductively attractive.

6. **Stop trying to understand, strategize and figure life out, which is masculine energy and stops all flow of creativity, intuition and support from Mother Earth.** Instead, open, all luscious, juicy and trusting as you surrender to the fact that it's supposed to be a mystery.

I love this one. It's supposed to be a mystery! How many of you like to know exactly how he'll make love to you, when he'll turn you over, when he'll come. You can count the thrusts while make a list for the grocery store. Yuck. No. We love surprises. We love it when we get a message, "Red dress. No panties. Pick you up at 8 pm." Holy crap, that turns me on. NONE of that fulfilling juiciness of life would be possible if we always had him figured out. None of the magic would be possible if we wasted all our energy trying to strategize what we need to do to get a certain result out of him. Now.

Letting go to the mystery takes courage. It takes, well, letting go. It takes jumping off the cliff and trusting. It risks that he may never call, never "pick you up at 8pm," and never surprise you in bed. So if he never shows up, it's HIS LOSS, my sweets!!! Yet being a sexy woman and attracting the attention you want DOESN'T happen when you're in control, trying to figure him out. That behavior repels him. An open, responsive, alert, juicy woman is JUST the thing he's looking for. See, he wants to win, wants to make you happy, wants to feel he's conquered you and you're enraptured. Surrender all your strategies and be open to the mystery and trust that a good man, a great man WILL worship a sexy goddess like you.

7. **Stop competing with the Universe, thinking that you know best.** Instead speak your truth, making an intention, and then surrender to a connection that has always and always will be there, a connection that brings your dreams or something even beyond your imagination and lays it gently at your feet.

So there's you. And then there's the Universe. Kind of small. Kind of big. What in heaven's name made you think you could compete with the Universe? I have led this life of insanity before and it's exhausting. Sexy women are sizzling and buzzing with yummy energy that has percolated from the well of Mother Earth inside. They're not exhausted. What if you took on the belief that the Universe is conspiring on your behalf? What if you decided to make your intentions or say your affirmations and then let go? I remember how I believed I had to say my affirmations all day every day or the Universe would forget. I was terrified to let go! I never let the tide go out so it could come back in! I never trusted that there was a flow in the Universe and I could ride the wave and be taken care of.

Women who aren't sexy are holding on for dear life. Sexy women have released their dreams at the shore and are dancing in the sand, optimistically waiting for their dreams, or something better, to be washed ashore at their feet. Sexy women trust that all is well. Sexy women know they can handle anything life gives them. Sexy women know how to let go and allow miracles to shower their life. Sexy women tend to be more orgasmic because they let go and gush their pleasure everywhere. Sexy women are the most courageous on the planet because it takes way more courage to let go than to hold on. Be willing to let go and feel a connection to Mother Earth in your body, in your heart, and watch it manifest in your life as attention, adoration, affection and love because a man, even though it may be subconsciously, wants to connect to all that is through your body and will be effortlessly attracted to you only when you've fully let go.

8. **Stop deflecting pleasure, joy, and success out of concern for what people will think and instead allow a love so deep, wide and pure that you feel like your heart will explode.** Then let it explode into deeper and wider love and see what life is like on the other side of fear.

Sexy women allow pleasure. Do you allow compliments? Do you allow in a humble yet joyful celebration of your success? Do you hold back your moans of delight as you savor the first bite of your meal? Do you watch to see if it's appropriate to be yourself when you make love for the first time? Every time you deflect the expression and experience of pleasure, it's as if the Universe says, "Ok, she's not really into this so let's turn it down a bit, less love, less affection, less adoration, less pleasure." And then the Universe gives it instead to the sexy women who let it all in! Now I'm not saying you should pull a Meg Ryan in the diner, but hey, why not?

The more you open the flood gates in your own authentic way, the more juice will come through those gates AND more reasons for juice to flow will manifest in your life.

Would it be so bad if you were experiencing so much joy and pleasure that your heart exploded? What's so bad about ecstasy? Bliss? Rapture? This is a simple thank you right into his eyes when he takes your groceries to the car (and nothing is more fulfilling to a man than to know he brings us pleasure). This is a joyful heartfelt hug and hello when you see your child. This is a loving and full-on body hug to your girlfriend telling her how gorgeous she looks today. This is uninhibited moans of pleasure when he's pleasing you. Sexy women don't hold back. Not only are they open to receiving, they are open to giving. They are a vessel through which life flows fully and they are beacons of light that attract noble men to ravish them to their depths.

9. **Stop being addicted to goals, affirmations, intentions and mantras, thinking that if you let go, God or the Universe will forget about you.** Start letting it all go, trusting the Universe heard you the first time and simply expect your miracle to come to you. Sexy women breathe in and out fully through their bellies. Notice that when you breathe shallowly, high up in your chest that you're in survival mode. Now imagine a goal or intention you have. Breathe it fully into your body and hold it there, savoring what that would feel like to have it, then exhale it ALL away, let go of it, see it moving far away past the farthest planet, see your cells being exhaled away as well, all that's left is your spirit at rest in the cosmos of everything. Practice breathing in that goal fully again, then exhaling it and you away again into the nothingness while you rest as everything, open and at peace. Notice if you're willing to let the goal and you go, of if you want to hang on and control the situation, attached to the outcome. Notice if you can totally let go and feel the connection to all that is. See

if you can sense that you are everything manifesting with ease as you allow the Universe to bring back your goal in divine time and expression.

Try intending that you give yourself and receive all the attention and affection you can receive, and breathe that in and hold it, relish it, savor it fully, then let it all go, let you go and rest as everything. At first it may seem scary or lonely or empty to let go of that which you crave so much, yet the practice of receiving it and letting it go will show you that more and more attention always comes. It builds trust with the flow of the Universe. AND after time you will notice that resting in everything feels JUST as full as breathing in attention. That's because all you really are is love. You are sensuality itself. You are sexuality itself. You are everything itself.

Before a first date, before you pick up the kids, before you sit down for dinner, before you make love, breathe a few breaths and open to receiving all your dreams, and let them all go and rest as everything while the Universe elegantly brings you a world beyond your dreams.

10. **Stop trying to be good, trying to make a difference, trying to do the right thing.** Know that you need do *nothing* but BE to be of value, to bring comfort to a child, to bring warmth to a lover, to bring tenderness to a friend, or to bring light to this world. Notice that when you try to be sexy you may get the result you want, yet now you'll have to keep remembering to do that and come from fear that if you don't, you'll lose him. Notice that when you try to be sexy, it sometimes backfires and he uses you for the night and leaves, or you somehow repel the guy you want and end up with the sleazy guy you don't want. Notice how devastated you feel in your heart when you really tried hard to be sexy and he ended up choosing someone else. Notice that when you tried to get attention and it didn't work you felt like you got the wind kicked out of you. That's because energetically you did.

Whenever we TRY to be sexy or get attention, we're literally prostituting our energy. We're giving it away in hopes of getting what we want yet always coming from an unbalanced place, a place of unworthiness, a place of hope that this time he'll like me, yet underneath we're waiting for the next rejection.

What if you just were yourself? What if you began to fill yourself up with all the practices you have and will find in this book and simply BE sexy? What if you stopped giving your power away by trying to get a result to happen and instead let that power magnify until you were so bright and luscious that a great, noble man wanted to sweep you off your feet? This takes trust, doesn't it? It takes a willingness to be in the gap while you are taking care of yourself, and perhaps not getting the attention you would from slimy men while you appreciate yourself, and literally appreciate your worth and attract that great man. It really comes down to drawing a line in the sand and saying, "I'm worth it. I will treat myself as such. I will enjoy myself as a sexy, sensual, succulent woman. I will appreciate myself with attention and affection. I will shift whatever beliefs and behaviors sabotage my power and I will positively expect to effortlessly and easily attract a great man, a great marriage, a great sex life and a great life."

And if you forget, re-read this book. Listen to the audios. Contact us for a power Intimacy Blindspot Breakthrough Session at www.AllanaPratt.com/connect. We have a proven digital online intimacy training called **HeartMates for Singles** that includes the **HeartMates Dating App** at no charge. If you're in a relationship then you can reignite your relationship with **HeartMates for Couples.** Stay connected and speak out. We are here for you! Under no circumstance are you ever alone, ever unloved, ever forgotten because now you have me. As I write this to you I'm already in love with you, championing your successes, your juiciness and your happiness.

CHAPTER 8

AMPLIFYING YOUR SEXY FACTOR

"I feel sexy most of the time, when I wear red fingernail polish,
when I wear high heels, when I'm dancing."

- Maria, 59

So now let's get you practicing! Reading is great and awareness is wonderful -- yet if you don't get these concepts into your body, nothing will change for you. Let the insights shift from mind awareness to bodily experience. If you apply these practices, embrace them as a new way of living, are willing to see what happens and stay unattached to the results, you will be floored and delighted with the results.

SIX MODERN TAKES ON ANCIENT PRACTICES FOR AMPLIFYING YOUR SEXY FACTOR

1. Open or close

Try this out. I know you've been reading for a while and hopefully we've created some affinity, yet pretend you don't know me at all right now.

Close yourself to me and what I have to say.

Close your mind, your body, your heart, your willingness, your openness.

Completely shut me out. What do you notice?

Probably that I'm bitchy, a know-it-all, and cold. You may think I'm an idiot, that this is a waste of time. Thank you.

Now, open to me, open your body, your heart, your mind, your willingness, your whole existence.

Open to what I have to say, open to my love for you and notice that I may seem warm, helpful, loving, encouraging and your champion.

Now, notice that the only thing that changed is YOU. Sexy women are open. They are open to others and they are open to themselves. They are open to the women they meet at work or at parties. They are open on a date or to their lover. Imagine consciously choosing to be open making love, talking to your lover, seeing your body in the mirror. Sexy women are inviting and magnetically attractive because they are open to life. It's like surrendering to the flow of the river -- trusting it will take you to your desired outcome, or even better.

2. Asking for help

Imagine you're at your most needy, overwhelmed, and panicked place ever. It's from here that you ask for help. Notice if you don't want to seem needy or weak, or if you don't want to feel like a burden. Notice if you don't want them to know you've given up. Now let that go. Imagine you're sitting in the most exquisite throne. Feel like you are a queen, responsible to the whole kingdom, overflowing with abundance, giving freedom of choice to all and then you ask for help.

Notice how you feel empowered, open, how you feel attractive and inviting to others to help you, how you know your kingdom flourishes because you've effectively delegated. Pretty powerful stuff, yes?

Now which do you think makes you look and feel sexier? Can you see how a man wouldn't want to serve you in the needy place and would pass you by for another woman? Can you see that in your queen place you've set him up to win to help you, serve you, attend to you? And yet you are so strong, capable and confident? Being willing to ask for help from the queen literally makes you attractive to men. AND it takes a load off you, which feels great, makes you shine more and be even sexier!!

A sexy woman allows a man to serve her, she rests into her worth and enjoys the way she can praise her hero for attending her. For years I felt uncomfortable letting a man help me as I was always keeping score: he did that so I owe him this. Deep down I never believed he did anything purely to please me. I truly believed he did it to get me to have sex, to build points so I wouldn't get mad if he screwed up. Deep down I had no idea that a man would get pleasure out of making me happy, that all I had to do was say thank you, how happy he made me, that he was my hero, that I am the luckiest woman alive and that those words MORE than made up for the effort he put forth. Now I understand that when I feel worthy and can open and allow a man to take care of me, cook for me, drive me places, pay for me, help me out with my son, trim my hedges (No..... I mean literally trim my hedges), that it actually brings a man joy to serve a true queen.

It's as if when the queen shows up, the noble man appears. If only an insecure little girl shows up posing as a queen, only sniveling idiots appear. Sorry, but true.

When a sexy woman can rest in her femininity, shower a man with praise and gratitude, truly express the pleasure she feels for his service, he'll want to do it again and again. What could be more fabulous for a man than to win at making us happy, radiant, juicy and open? Women, we can inspire our men to serve us forever. First know you're worth it, second open your heart and let it in, third praise him while feeling and expressing your pleasure. Be willing to have life be THAT good.

3. Get out of your head and into your heart

I've spoken about this earlier, but now let's talk about how you really feel it. First, imagine you've cut off your body and you're just a head. Now begin to think about your to-do list. Quicken the pace to that of a race, start strategizing, manipulating situations, keeping to your agenda, not open to support and feeling alone and overwhelmed. Do do do. Never enough, fast enough, good enough. Now imagine you are only a body. Feel into your open chest, into your relaxed shoulders, into your heart, breathing it open with each breathe. Relax and soften deeper past your heart, into your stomach, totally let go and open. Sink down into your pelvis, open and relax your vagina, open and present yourself splayed open and connected into deep, dark, moist, wet, powerful Mother Earth. Sinking down, allow Mother Earth's energy to fill you with your every breath. You're as wide as forest, as deep as the ocean, as fierce as a tornado, as calm as a gentle breeze blowing through a field of wheat at sunset. YOU are everything. You are intuition itself. Notice that you feel calm, empowered, full. Know that in this space you are so magnetically attractive and sensual. Now the practice is staying in this open space when driving, when talking to coworkers, when connecting with your lover, when listening to a friend, when going to the gym, when making love. Watch the miracles that you attract when in this energy. Watch in wonder as you speak poetry or come up with amazing solutions to problems. Watch how you orgasm deeper than ever before and connect profoundly heart-to-heart with your lover. Watch as you feel unstoppable and free in the world.

4. Dissolving the permanent kegel

This one's funny to me because it shows how unconsciously panicked I was walking around all day with my vagina clenched in what doctors call a kegel. So tighten your jaw, your shoulders, cave in your chest, tighten your stomach and clench your perma-kegel (vagina — like you have to pee) then imagine introducing yourself to someone. Imagine trying to dance. Imagine trying to make love. Can't you just feel the orgasm would be very clitoral, all contracted and shallow?

Now then, concentrically relax each part of your body I mentioned. Relax your jaw, your shoulders, open your chest, breathe deeply, relax your stomach, soften your kegel, breathe through your pelvis until your vagina is fully open, imagining your heart and brain and lungs all reside in the pelvis, noticing yes, this is our sexual center, yet it's also our creative center. It's also where intuition lives and where connection to the divine resides for a woman. Now imagine introducing yourself to another. Imagine dancing. Imagine making love. Worlds apart, yes? Our society has shamed us for the feelings we get when we live in our pelvis. We haven't been taught that if you send those energetic sensations downward they become sexual and delicious. And if you send the energy upwards it becomes creativity manifested as our gifts to the world. So breathe in your pelvis. Dissolve the perma-kegel and know the true meaning of "Sexy women are juicy from the inside out."

5. Bringing home your little girl

This one's very moving to me. When a woman is sad, angry or afraid and stays in the victim cycle unable to forgive herself, she will continually attract less-than-noble men, be sentenced to sabotaging her happiness and be totally disconnected from being sexy. I know this because this is where I came from.

Imagine I'm looking directly in your eyes. I look beyond everything right to the place where you are hiding your anger, fear or sadness. Find that place I'm looking into -- the place within your body that you feel the contraction of emotion -- your heart, your throat, your stomach, etc. Begin to breathe into this place as if this is the only part of your body that exists. Now imagine there is a dark room inside that part of your body and your higher self goes in. She finds a part of you there, a younger you, a scared, angry or sad little girl part of you. The room and the little girl are in black and white. Her back is turned away from you. Let your higher self talk to her. Tell her that you're here to validate her, hear her, be with her, not change her at all, but simply understand her. Ask her for forgiveness for abandoning her, ignoring her, denying her, making her wrong, trying to make her go away. Tell her you see her fully and love her unconditionally no matter how she feels and no matter how long she feels that way. Tell her you will always protect her from now on. Imagine sending a rainbow- colored stream of love from your higher self's heart to the little girl's heart. As you do see her timidly turn toward you, change from black and white to color and turn around and look you right in the eye. Your higher self smiles, opens her arms and the little girl runs into them and you hold her there, welcoming her home, rocking her, resting in this union, allowing tears to heal everything. Tell her you'll hold her until the emotion passes. Be willing to meet her nightly for a week if that's what it takes.

Know that until we heal this little girl, she's in front of our sexiness and we show up as needy or controlling to men. Know that having our little girl where she's supposed to be, with us, behind us, safe, playing and at peace, will set free our full mature sexual power and sensual expression.

Note: This exercise is too confronting for many women. I personally had to have someone guide me through it several times as I met all my girls, the sad one, the angry one and the scared one. If you need guidance, contact me for group coaching or a private "Emotional Integration" session or a "Sexual Karma Clearing" session.

6. Letting go of poison -- anger release

While I love doing this in a sacred workshop space where we all let 'er rip, I can tell you what to do in the privacy of your own home or way out in nature where no one can hear you. You'll want to be able to hit pillows and scream obscenities. This is about getting rid of stuck anger in the body and mind that is holding back the very connection we're longing for with men, and is making us sick, dull, nasty and crabby from the inside out. I want you to put on some really wild heavy metal music or intense drumming music and begin to have a full-on tantrum. You may start to laugh yet this is serious stuff. I believe my mom ultimately died from all the anger she kept in her body that ate away her liver with cancer. I want you to stamp your feet, yell in gibberish, whine and moan, shake out your body. I want you to hit the crap out of a pillow, take a foam bat and knock the daylights out of the couch. It feels amazing and you will instantly feel better. When you want to end -- DON'T STOP, keep on shaking or hittting or screaming to one more song. Normally there's more. No longer will you cut people off, interrupt, be righteous, be so controlling, hold grudges, feel like a victim, snap at people, project your unprocessed anger on another. By doing this you are making the choice to not be right but rather, to be happy. You could stay right which means you keep your anger (poison) in your body, eating away at your own soul while you give away your power by stewing over the past.

The choice to be happy often requires letting something go -- in mind and in body -- for the sake of your own happiness, and you will also need to become present to the magic of the moment. Women who are courageous enough to let go of the past, face their demons and release them, are powerfully sexy women. It means you can follow the spectrum of love from the light into the dark, from tender sweetness to loving ravishment. Your sexiness factor will be off the charts. And you will be free.

Here's another common question from one of our sisters:

"I've never valued my femininity, was told to "man up"
even as a little girl, to do things myself, to never need a man,
and while I admit I'm jealous of women who make men drool,
honestly I don't respect them either.
I mean I'll let him open the door, but I'll never need him."

Okay, let's get clear, real and to the point. Do you really want a man who drools? Or do you want a man who respects you yet gets a little weak in the knees when he sees you? One that makes you feel gorgeous when he looks at you?

Are you happy to know that you can do things yourself? I hope so! I think it feels fabulous to know all that we can accomplish and endure. And yet, are you tired? At all lonely? You say you're jealous and yet don't respect these women. I encourage you to shift that and learn from these classy women who are in the space where a man supports her, adores her, attends to her, takes care of her. I want you to make her your teacher, your mentor, your guide. She simply has awakened a capacity inside of you that is still dormant. She doesn't have something you don't. Perhaps you're more adept in areas she'd be jealous of! The point is she really doesn't need him to open doors or do much for her, I imagine. She ALLOWS him. Big difference.

You don't need a man. Yet he needs to feel needed, important, like a hero, able to win, to support you, to make a difference, to feel useful, to elicit a smile from you, a luxurious sigh, a soft touch, a temptresses wink ... oh, the list goes on. Use the energy you WOULD have used getting much needed rest, enjoy writing, call a friend, fill up your tank in ways that brings you joy and creates more radiance in your life. Then you'll shine even brighter and he'll want to support you more!

Receiving support and pleasure is courageous work! Seriously! It means opening your heart wider and wider, knowing indeed you ARE worthy! I say enjoy the process, sister. You can do it.

Here's another valid question from a smart, successful busy woman:

> *"How do you honestly do these practices when working*
> *sixty to eighty hours a week. I don't get paid to relax.*
> *I get acknowledged and praised and paid to work."*

You make a brilliant point. So the question really is "Are you happy?" If you are happy and on fire living your purpose working sixty to eighty hours a week, and you're happily married, adoring of your partner, then we don't have an issue! My off the charts manager runs multimillion dollar companies and LOVES it! She's madly in love, she and her partner are highly creative in the times they cherish and spend together, she embraces beauty as a part of her world, her dress, her environment, her clients, her lover, her child. She looks for the beauty, she creates the beauty. She finds time to nourish herself with ways SHE loves, with a book in a bag on her surfboard.

So you may only need one humdinger of practice and you're good to go!

The question is if you're NOT happy, sister ... then what?

If you work to get praise and acknowledgement, then you're created a life where you're only feel enough if you keep working.

Where else do you feel praised and acknowledged? For just being you? For just being alive? If this hasn't been cultivated yet, you need to do some inner work.

If you're single this is even MORE reason to do this inner work because with the exception of a male gold digger, you're not going to find a man who is only turned on by your accomplishments. He's going to want to be with you, be able to win with you, be able to support you in some fashion, be it his killer foot rubs or the way you snuggle into his arms after a long day.

And that's going to take courage to open, to show you aren't needy but you have desires, to put healthy boundaries around your schedule for self-care, for dating, for a social life, for downtime.

If I was your mentor I would recommend a full day intensive with me. I imagine you're pretty wound up and would take longer than an hour to open up, trust, let go, really sink in, feel, reveal truths, heal and get clear on what you really, really want, then go about shifting your life step-by-step to create what you want and the space for him to show up while enjoying your career.

You have to decide if he's worth it, if YOU'RE worth it, if you're willing to get clear on your dream and allow it to happen.

CHAPTER 9

SENSUAL RADIANCE

"I feel sexy when I'm all dressed up
and my fiancé's eyes are only on me,
because I'm feeling courageous, passionate and loving."

- Brandy, 29

The next nine solutions I have to offer work for all women –
single, married, mothers, stepmoms – all the time because we are
truly all the same on the inside!

NINE SAVVY SOLUTIONS
FOR THE MODERN SEXY WOMAN

PART 1 - HOW TO BE RAVISHING WITH YOUR MAN

1. Adorn yourself to feel like a goddess

How much passion would you connect to if I asked you -- how
would you dress if you were meeting the divine masculine
today? This reminds you that you are a luscious goddess at
your core. Beautiful clothes that honor and celebrate your

expression can put you in the mood, dissolve neediness and enhance self-confidence. In all your glory and gorgeousness, watch him be attracted to your sexy radiance. Watch how you have courage to ask for what you want! Whether it's shopping or a clothes swap with your friends, give yourself the gift of adorning your body in clothes that make you feel lovely. Waiting 'til you lose those pounds to feel good about yourself means you're withholding self-love today! Self-love brings clarity and creativity! Decide today that you are a goddess and adorn yourself accordingly. LET GO of all clothes that make you feel like anything less than stunning and succulent. Before you know it you will have found your signature style ... the outfits that make you feel radiant!

2. Live from your vagina

Notice that we're in our heads all day long!!! I've talked to you about HOW to move your awareness into your vagina. Now let's put it into action! What if in a moment of question, challenge, misunderstanding, frustration with your man, you didn't try to figure it out in your brain? (Because that's just a file folder of past challenges and solutions, and this is new so how can it help you now truly?) So instead breathe into your hips as if they were your brain, your lungs, your heart and your intuition. What FEELS right? What would LOVE say through your vagina to your man? If you can find a few minutes to close the door to your office or go into the bathroom or wiggle around in your car seat, just move your hips wider than you normally do, breathe into all tight or anxious areas and ask your body to answer. You'll be amazed that you know EXACTLY what to do. It might take courage to follow through, but you'll be in your power. Come from loving kindness, be straight, be unattached and act from your feminine power center.

Note: It may seem obvious but is worth emphasizing that this practice is not just for interactions with your lover – it also works beautifully with coworkers, friends, kids and yourSELF! Stop reacting and respond from your vagina and watch your power, peace and pleasure soar!

3. Feed him by hand

From the bottom of my heart, I want to thank all the women who have come before me. The women who were burned at the stake, who marched in picket lines, who've been murdered, raped, jailed, humiliated, imprisoned and controlled. I thank every woman who fought for our right to be educated, to vote, to be paid equally, to be safe, and to be honored. I pray for every woman in this very moment who is being oppressed physically, emotionally, mentally or spiritually.

There are moments when I write that I feel their fury, and their passion. I feel them championing you and me, fully embracing our feminine power, fully validating our right to be sexually expressed and sensually free. I feel them assuring me that our greatest power is to bring love, light, juiciness and radiance to this world. We are not to feel sorry for them. They willingly paved the way and celebrate our courage to shine, to honor our beauty inside and out, to unite as sisters and savor being a woman. I say that because feeding a man by hand seems so primal, so simple, so pure and for some, perhaps degrading.

For years women couldn't be free to do such a thing because we had to fight so hard to be respected as more than just the one who stayed home with the kids. I still experience the concern that if I let him open the door for me, he'll think I'm incapable, an idiot, weak, or easily taken advantage of. So be sure when you read this that you have let go of any reaction to injustices of the past. They are true ... and they are gone for the most part. What truly honors the past the most is being about to hold your self-worth intact WHILE giving of your sensual gifts. There aren't too many great role models for us.

Perhaps Sophia Loren, perhaps Veronica Franco in Dangerous Beauty give you that essence of being strong, honored, yet sultry, and seductive. Being sexy is really about living life sensually, taking time to be present to all your senses.

So feed your lover by hand. Choose exotic, savory, exquisite-smelling foods or simply make his favorite meal. Take time to make him ache for the food as he'll ache to taste you. Also YOU be an example of sensuality by eating a stalk of asparagus or a chocolate covered strawberry in a way that would embarrass his friends yet completely turn him on. Think of yourself as a sexual artisan gifting him with your sensual seduction.

PART 2 - HOW TO BE A HEARTFELT SEXY SISTER WITH YOUR GIRLFRIENDS

4. Be naughty with the girls

I'm not proposing you get into any trouble that you'd feel guilty about in the morning. I think the whole "What Happens in Vegas, Stays In Vegas" is a bunch of BS for people who don't have the courage to face what's not working in their lives in an honoring way and shift it, and instead project their lack of living their truth into destructive behaviors under the guise of sin city. Weak. I'm talking about something much more delicious, completely empowering and a way to not only deepen connection with girlfriends but also gift the results to your man while expanding your joy and self-esteem. Strong. So there were times when women prepared each other for their wedding night, where they taught each other the art of sexual play and sensual expression.

Here's an opportunity to create that same energy with your girlfriends.

What I want you to do in a sensual, naughty way is to feed each other chocolate. Draw the drapes, put on that music from the movie "9 1/2 Weeks" and help each other learn how to receive pleasure. The one who's eating closes her eyes (you could even blindfold her with velvet or satin material) and as she eats the variety of chocolate offerings (make them hot, cold, crunchy, pudding, ones that pop liqueur in the inside are fun!), she is to express her pleasure. The one feeding should encourage her to expand her capacity to express and receive pleasure by telling her "more, louder, deeper, naughtier, more orgasmic, more tender, more powerful, etc." Just have fun going crazy in the living room with your friends experiencing chocolate. Then go out on the town and notice that you are MAGNETS to men. They want a woman who feels pleasure in her body because HE'LL probably feel pleasure in there too!

You can be creative and ritualistic and meet under the full moon and dance with the wet grass between your toes. Go to the spa together and melt into the hot tub, share your journey with each other, enjoy how good it feels to be heard by a sister who believes in you. Fill yourself up then return home, telling your man why he's your hero. Or if you haven't met your man yet, imagine talking to him in your journal, or dancing for him by candle light, giving your gift to the divine masculine who will bring your real man to your life.

5. Release energy drains

Have you heard of the Goddess Kali? She will cut off a man's head if he's not living his truth, his deepest purpose. She's bold, takes no prisoners, will stop at nothing but the truth. I invite you to explore this archetype in you because she will tell you where you're spending time with draining acquaintances or doing things out of obligation instead of truth. When you find one of these areas, a draining person or a commitment you made that you're no longer committed to, be willing to complete it and move on. There is no cookie cutter way to do this but it's more about who you're being than what you say.

First, internally forgive yourself for not honoring your own boundaries. Forgive the other person too, yet acknowledge that you were the one who put yourself in this position, so take responsibility and be kind to yourself. When you feel at peace, be kind but firm and say "I'm honored, yet, no, thank you." Or "I apologize for any inconvenience this may cause, yet I am no longer a fit for this project and I am completing my participation today." Clean up whatever you can clean up by finding a replacement and finishing your work, because the sooner you stop draining your energy trying to be liked or not disappoint another, the sooner that very same energy can start radiating from you as a sexy, sensual woman. Your energy is precious and you are always at choice whether to give it away and avoid confrontation, or speak your truth with honesty and kindness and create a life where people honor your time and energy.

6. Fulfill yourself no matter what

Have you ever met someone who was thinner, richer, had a hot boyfriend, had the best clothes, had a better job, was happier, seemed more confident, got more attention, was sexier than you, and you secretly hated her? Didn't it give you a sick feeling in your stomach or stir you up and get you pissed off? I totally get it. Been there. Yet, have you ever noticed that when you're newly in love, just got a new haircut, just got promoted or landed a new client, when you're feeling hot in a new outfit, walk into a room with a man on your arm, are asked for your number, that you feel great?

Here's the thing ... in the first case, we're giving all our power away to others, comparing ourselves and making them somehow responsible for our sorry lives. In the second, we're moving in the right direction because we're happier -- yet again we're letting external circumstances dictate our level of self-worth and happiness. Notice that there is no reason to be envious or jealous of others when your life works. And also notice that there's no reason to give your power away to an external circumstance making you happy when you're already at peace inside. Sexy women aren't competitive. Sexy women don't derive their self-confidence from the outside.

All the internal practices I've given you are to make you invincible, limitless, empowered, and radiant from the inside out. THEN when you buy that purse or celebrate your win at work or the new guy it will be humble, almost like you knew it was going to happen — no need to show off and no need to be worried that it could go away, leaving you alone and feeling unworthy. Sexy women are somehow just as able to savor a sunset in the back of a pickup truck in a farm field as they are on a yacht in the Mediterranean. AND they will attract men in both places to brighten their world.

So "Fulfill Yourself No Matter What" is about gratefully seeing other women who may push your buttons as reminders that there is a dormant part of you that needs to wake up. Thank your sister for showing you it's time to get healthy, to get back to your love of swimming in the ocean, to take more time to nourish yourself from the inside out, to find a more fulfilling career. Do what it takes to create the life you love. Be willing to have a life practice of finding fulfillment in the moment so you can be a profound listener, unconditionally loving and free of judgment with all you meet. Now that is sexy. Sexy that lasts. Sexy that attracts a GOOD man.

PART 3 - HOW TO BE A TRUE SENSUAL LOVE LIGHT IN THE WORLD

7. Give yourself permission to meet your needs

There is nothing sexy about a dry, crackly, bitchy, whining woman. Notice when you're operating on empty and ask yourself where do you get the biggest bang for your buck to fill your tank? Schedule it NOW and REGULARLY, as this is the catalyst for you being happy on a consistent basis. Treat this appointment with yourself like you'd treat an important meeting ... because it IS!

What is the big attraction to putting everyone else in front of us? Why does getting attention for our victim story seem so appealing when we're the one suffering? What will it take for you to make YOU number one and fill yourself to overflowing so you can smolder in your sexual sassiness, enjoy being a woman and attract all the attention and affection you can stand from a willing and noble man? Imagine the activity that brings you home to your pelvis, makes you open and relax and trust that everything is working out as it should be. Is it the beach, a hike, a massage, a bath? Some like cleaning the house, others like masturbating, some like baking and other need to have their toes and nails done weekly. There is no right answer, only right for you. Make it a regular part of your life and notice how much sexier you feel when you treat yourself like the sensual goddess you are! Also, set an intention for this time for you to be the space for divine guidance, inspiration and answers to be revealed. See what magic unfolds.

8. Don't buy into excuses

I'm as guilty of this as the next woman. Fortunately, what I've learned is that when I really come from "everything is perfectly unfolding and I have all that I require," I am able to find ways to live fully now no matter what. So have you ever heard someone say, "I'll be sexy once I've lost the forty pounds?" Or, "I'll focus on a great relationship after I work hard for a few more years and prove myself?" Or, "I need to wait 'til the kids are grown to be fulfilled again in my marriage sexually?" I say those are all excuses. Granted, being creative enough to find a way to meet your desires now will take focus and persistence, but I promise you, nothing — absolutely nothing — is in the way of you being sexy right now and having the love and attention you deserve. Really decide that you CAN have what you want, you ARE willing to make changes, you are OPEN to a miracle and you're READY to be happier.

You want to feel sexier? Great. How do you feel when you're sexy? Succulent, sassy, powerful, juicy, open and full. Find a way to feel that way, the essence of sexy, today! This may sound ridiculous, yet I love to dress kind of funky and find the local Little India and begin a sensual adventure of trying on saris, buying bangles, eating delicious curries, drinking masala tea, wearing extra eyeliner. I feel very sexy and just energetically I'm sending out a signal to the Universe that I'm worth being adored. Honestly, I've never met a man there, yet I've come home to three messages from men on my answering machine while there. Remember, our desires are really our yearning for an experience. Sure, I want to feel sexy, but really I want the experience of juiciness, openness, adventure. And THOSE are available every day, everywhere, in every way. Start BEING a sexy woman.

9. Start your day being enough

For years I portrayed the illusion to the world that I am a confident woman, yet on the inside I believed that I was never enough. I could never receive a compliment from another without denying it or sending one right back. I could never be held by a man without thinking, "He's probably done, bored, what should I do for him now?" I began each day like a war against time to accomplish enough that I could say I made a difference, I helped someone, I proved something. It was exhausting and I could never win the battle. I would lay my head down to sleep, still rehashing how I could have done something better, how I could have said something different so he would have liked me enough to call me, I could have worn a different outfit so she wasn't prettier than me. Insanity, but that was my life.

Now, by doing all the practices I've shared with you in my own time at my own pace, my life began to shift. I realized my behavior and had a really good cry about it. I cried for days, actually. I practiced letting girlfriends hold me as I cried. I practiced affirming before I got out of bed each morning that "I am enough." We need not accomplish superwoman deeds to be worthy, cherished and accepted. Just being alive you are a gift! Imagine the feeling in your body of having lived a day full of delight and begin your day with that feeling, get dressed with that feeling, interact with others from an "it's already done and it went beautifully" feeling. Sexiness isn't always trying to do better. Sexy is luxuriating in the now, savoring the moment, inhaling life. Remember you are a shining light of succulence and heartfelt radiance. It's not "seeing is believing." It's BELIEVING is seeing. Believe you are a sexy woman and act as if it's true. Your actions will align and you will breathe your glorious worth in and out, opening your heart to the attention and adoration you deserve.

CHAPTER 10

CENTERED THROUGH MAYHEM

"I feel sexy when a gentleman opens the door for me,
when I see how being feminine has grown
my children and grandchildren.
When I dance I feel free
like there are no worries in the world."

- Angie, 65

While everything I've been suggesting has worked for me and countless women just like you, I often get asked how to "keep your sexy" when negativity strikes. Great question, because if we allow outside circumstances to dictate our moods, we're giving our power away. If we drain away our well-earned sensual energy by reacting to someone who's simply dumping their bad mood into our space, we also suffer because now we are back at square one having to tend our inner fire again. Learning how to go with the flow, have healthy boundaries and protect our feminine essence is essential for a powerful, sexy woman.

FOUR SECRETS TO STAY SENSUAL, CENTERED AND TRUSTING WHILE MANEUVERING THROUGH MAYHEM

Feeling versus Reacting

As women we really are so busy, we very rarely take time to listen deeply to how we are truly feeling. Instead we may use unrelated disappointments here and there to really unload our grievances -- judge other women for getting more attention than us, project our envy onto other women who appear sexier than us, etc. My advice would be to have a bath once a week for the sole purpose of checking in -- do you need to really cry? Do you want to journal if you're confused? Do you want to write some creative thoughts down and follow your dreams? Do you want to go through each area of your body and bless it with gratitude? Do you want to stop thinking altogether and simply practice BEING? You see, we all have the same twenty-four hours a day to develop our sex appeal from the inside out. If you don't schedule YOU time, it doesn't happen and that inner voice can't guide and encourage you. When you take YOU time, your sexual expression and sensual freedom becomes a natural unfolding of the real YOU.

Meltdowns

To be a sensual woman in the face of chaos it takes a lot. And yet see if you can open your heart no matter what's happening. Let's say your coworker is having a meltdown, or your boss has lost his lid, or your man is ranting about the injustices of the world, or your child is having a tantrum at the store. You're feeling frustrated, uncomfortable, maybe even embarrassed. In that moment, instead of judging, resisting and reacting to outside circumstances, imagine inhaling into Mother Earth and exhaling out the top of your head all your frustrations. Open your body and remember you have all you require. Breathe again and affirm that you can handle it. Remember nothing is personal even if someone is projecting onto you. Breathe and know that inside is your intuition, and you can't go wrong from a place of love. All you need to ask is "What would love do now?"

Maybe you need to remove yourself and let the person calm down. Maybe they simply want to be heard and feel incomplete with their past conversations with you. Maybe the fact that you're not biting diffuses the situation and they take responsibility right away and move on. Regardless, you didn't lose your cool, you didn't lose your power, you didn't lose your sensual connection to Mother Earth, and you're still open, alive and powerful and have all your juiciness left to attract the attention and affection you deserve.

Wandering Eyes

Let's say you're in a restaurant with your man. A beautiful woman walks by and you watch his eyes stray. You happen to feel overweight that day, you haven't slept well, you haven't had time for YOU in forever, and inside you are either boiling or hopeless. In that moment, you have two choices. One: you can judge her, shut down, get snippy, and we know how the rest of the night will go – no affection, no attention, no sex, and you'll be miserable perhaps for days AND you're scared now every time you go out with him that it will happen again. Or, Two: open and say thank you, sister. She is your mirror. You are a radiant woman, too. Let her remind you to take even better care of yourself. See if you can forgive him, forgive her and simply love yourself. See if you can feel the Universe's way of saying "Gotcha!" because spirit wants you to take more YOU time so that you're overflowing with juiciness. Open, shine and watch how your man responds to you the rest of the evening when you didn't freak out.

Perhaps with an open heart, begin talking about what you like about him. Then ask what he likes about you. Ask for his direction in an area of your life where you want clear masculine intuition. Ask him when he thinks you're the most radiant — after yoga? After a night out with the girls? When you get your hair done? After working on certain projects that bring out your talents? I bet he'll be mesmerized by your willingness to be proactive in your self-care and will support you in doing so. I imagine that night will be far more steamy than if you'd shut down. Sexy women aren't necessarily sexy 24/7. We ebb and flow like the tides, we can always expand more each day and we can always love ourselves unconditionally when we've strayed away from our true, natural, sensual nature and lovingly bring ourselves home.

Silly Is Sexy

I think there is nothing sexier than a woman unafraid to be silly, be herself, be wild if she feels wild, be dorky if she's feeling dorky, and be sultry if she's feeling sultry. She's free and that is completely sexy. So in my house, I want to raise a well- mannered boy, yet in the midst of all my rules, there needs to be some silliness for my son to go wild and for me to let go! We liked to dance to Reggae on our coffee table when he was little. We'd have dinner in the playhouse or under the table in a fort and eat mac and cheese with our fingers. One time we had a shaving cream fight in the back yard and washed off in the kiddy pool. We sometimes would go to the grocery store in our pajamas taking his stuffed animal bear along for the ride. All I knew in each of those moments was that I felt free and we had fun. Yet what I didn't know was that my boyfriend at the time found us hysterical and found me very sexy. You see, sexy is being free in your body. If I'm free in life, I'll be free in bed! Men love all our flavors and a predictable woman is boring and passed over for a sexier more adventurous one. So love yourself and the moment exactly as it is. Loosen up and have some fun!

Now here's one real world question that came through that I want to address:

"My husband is never stepping up, never following through, never keeping his word on a regular basis.

I have to do everything and I'm exhausted, resentful and wanting to leave him."

I hear your frustration and exhaustion. I'd feel the same way if I had to do everything. I'd want to leave him too. I wonder how long it's been like this, their whole marriage? I'm wondering if she is the main bread winner? Or she runs the household? Or both? Giving blame gets us nowhere, and facts are facts, let's begin by reminding you that you have a choice. You don't HAVE to do everything, you choose to do everything because I doubt he gets it done on time, or correctly, yes? While it will cause chaos in the short term, I want you first to get really clear on what you want to do and what you want him to do.

Just make a list on the fridge that reads "It Makes Me Super Happy To" then list your responsibilities and then another list that states "It Makes Me Super Happy that John Does" and list whatever it is that you'd like him to do. Men don't change until it's a problem for THEM.

Then only do what you feel in your deepest heart is fair, balanced and cooperative to do. If that means garbage doesn't get taken out, get out those air fresheners. If that means dinner is cereal, so be it. If that means his towel stays on the floor gathering mildew, so be it.

What I'm hearing, while you're valid and accurate, is a victim. You're playing along and exhausting yourself. Now your biggest job is to stay as unemotional as possible around him. STOP ENGAGING in fights, whining, blaming or even heavy sighs. No rolling eyes either. Go out to the backyard and stamp around to get your anger out, go to your room and scream in a pillow, but getting angry AT him gives him fuel that you're hysterical and nothing will change. It will defer the issue and make it your fault.

Play logical, not dumb. "Oh, well you didn't put your clothes in the laundry basket so I thought that meant they were clean."

You will be amazed at how quickly his behavior will change with those things that really mean something to him. With his behaviors that haven't changed with things that really mean something to you, get even more creative on how you can respond (not react) to somehow make it a problem for him.

I heard a story about one woman whose husband spoke in a condescending way about her job when they went out for dinner with his professional friends. They had fights about it, she'd withhold sex about it, she'd stick up for herself at these dinners. Nothing changed his behavior.

Then she decided to stay calm and take an action that would be a problem to him. She excused herself to the bathroom and told the waiter that her husband was so impressed with his service and the restaurant that he wanted to buy every table in the restaurant the best bottle of wine in the house. She said NOTHING on the way driving home. He never spoke condescendingly about her again. He simply said, "I get it. I won't make fun of you again. Just promise me you'll never do that again."

Lastly, use your new found downtime, while you're NOT picking up after him or blaming him, to begin some of the nourishing, sensual, feminine practices in this book. Your capacity to stay calm, feel deserving, and respond not react, depend on them.

CHAPTER 11

SUCCULENCE
WITH CLASS

"I feel sexy when I'm in my power and when I love my body."

- Miranda, 40

Have you ever heard a friend say that affirmations just don't work for her? Well I know what she means. Even if you say, "I'm sexy" all day long and yet underneath it, you haven't done the practices you've learned about in my book, you end up subconsciously sabotaging yourself all day long, which is tremendously disheartening.

And yet, once your foundation is clear, you're in your body and out of your head, affirmations and new behaviors can skyrocket your success with your sexual appeal and sensual satisfaction. That's why I'm leaving these practices until now because they will require very little effort from you and go a LONG way in attracting attention and affection because you will be the most radiant, luscious creature around!

10 SIMPLE YET PROFOUND PRACTICES
TO UNLEASH YOUR SUCCULENCE WITH CLASS

Delegate

It's impossible to be sexy when you're frazzled. I am hereby giving you permission to ask for help so that your kingdom thrives. Yes, my queen, I want you to consider shopping for groceries online, and once a week hiring the kid next door to wash and fold your laundry, take out the garbage and go to the post office for you. Consider hiring a virtual assistant to help you make appointments, research travel, send out your holiday cards. Seriously, how many hours would that buy you a week for YOU to use as sacred time to nourish your sexy soul, Sister? Feel the guilt and hop in the bath anyway. Take your journal and answer the question, "Why do I choose to live my dreams?" and see what your higher self answers.

Dyad Communication

You can't be sexy if there's an elephant in the living room, unless of course you're draped over its back in a stunning sequined number. But seriously, one of the best ways I know to be sexy is to face areas in your life that you are resisting and handle them. Scary? Well normally, yes. That's because whenever you have THE conversation it always ends up in a fight, right? So how about this: sit with a loved one, husband, best friend and make room for truth, healing and transformation in your relationships and life. You may begin this practice sacredly with lighting a candle and bowing. Just be sure to ask the questions with an open heart with the intention to understand and find healing in the relationship. Your intention goes a long way.

Once you've heard your partner's answer, the only response you may offer is "Thank you." No opinions, no "but, but!", not even non-verbal feedback like smiling if you like the communication or frowning if you don't. Just practice listening and that's it. Go back and forth with each set of three questions in a row for forty minutes. And then bless the communication you've had, and release it forever. Let it go. You are never to speak again about what you heard. And this way, each time you come together for a dyad, it's brand new to both of you. This is to bridge a line of safe, honoring communication between you two. When I first began doing dyads, I really wanted men to like me and while I also wanted more female friends, I was competitive and insecure about who was sexier than me. My teachers at the time helped me turn my "kinks into art" and inspired my path to empower women to open to their magnificent, sexual radiance.

I'm sure you'll agree that words create worlds. Questions open doors to new realities. Dyads are used in my HeartMates Intimacy Training, and in my Dating App. Questions are the foundation of my group and private work and retreats. YOU have the answers inside. I help facilitate the integration of your emotional triggers so you can HEAR your truth and awaken your deepest essence and knowing.

A longer list of dyad questions is found in the Rituals of Intimacy chapter in my book, **7 Steps to Manifest Your Beloved, While Staying True To Yourself.**

"Tell me something you like about me." (Creates affinity)

"Tell me something you think we align on." (Affirms that you're on the same team)

"Tell me something you think I should know." (Allows a safe space to tell the truth, the hurt beneath the anger, the pain of not being respected, etc.)

Teach people to respect time for YOU

How are we supposed to find our sexy, sensual succulence and reignite our passions when we're operating on fumes and overwhelm? Healthy boundaries are essential and yet you may have trained your world that you'll always be there for them and if you try to take some time back for you, they give you the guilt trip or complain. Breathe. They are addicted to you and your energy! Forgive them for their response and forgive yourself for giving away too much of you before you filled yourself up! THEN create a plan for when you need YOU time and present it to the co-workers, boyfriend, husband, children in a way that makes them see that if they become your heroes in supporting you in this, you will be able to gift them with patience, creativity, sensuality, etc.

Years ago, my son knew he had to wait until "Seven Zero Zero" to wake me up because I was finding patience and kindness for him. This empowered him to help ME find it and he felt like my hero while I used the time for a bath, workout, meditation or simply sleep! You could explain to your man that "it would mean a lot to me if/it would make me really happy if you would make dinner tonight so that I could go to yoga and find my juiciness and yumminess for you." Then enjoy your yoga class and be sure to enjoy a sultry night of love-making when you get home. In no time at all he'll be asking, "Isn't tonight yoga, honey?" as he remembers to get you out the door on time for class because he's learned how to win!

Dance for yourself

I've written about the power of dance in my life and as a method I suggest for you, for meeting repressed shame, for connecting with spirit, and for turning your man on. I want you to know that as women, it's very effective to let go of stress through movement in our hips because we store so much emotion there. Dance and move your hips wider than you normally do, breathe into all tight or anxious areas including your forehead, shoulders, stomach, vagina. Release self-judgments and commit to love yourself exactly as you are. Dance because you're alive, because you're a woman, a lover. Dance with the intention to get out of your head and back into your body where all your intuition lives. This way you become full from the inside out. This dissolves neediness and attachment and makes you into an invitation for him to shower you with attention. Dance and let go!

100% responsibility for your life

It's hard to be sexy when someone is pushing your buttons and doing it successfully! The bottom line in every situation is that the other person has triggered something in you. If someone says you're a bad cook and you know you're a total gourmet, you kind of look at them with disbelief yet it doesn't hurt your feelings, right? Yet, if someone says you're not sexy enough and you know that you're trying your best you blow your top or drop in a heap of tears! Gotcha! Know that if anything pushes your buttons, as much as we may resist admitting it, there is a shred of truth in what they say. It's your job to dismiss yourself, and forgive them because they've only cast a light on an unresolved issue. Then be kind to yourself. You've done your best in your unconsciousness, your avoidance, your denial, your being right or being a victim. This is a new moment that you can take 100% responsibility for. Own it, acknowledge it without self-judgment, forgive yourself and extend love to this part of you that is most likely scared, sad and angry. See what feelings come up to be released, again, without judgment.

There is always wisdom on the other side of resistance. Let go, forgive, feel, accept what is … insights, new choices, new boundaries, new experiences ... wisdom is at hand. And what's great is that it's been inside you all along. You may come to a place where you can even thank the other person for bringing this to your attention. To me, that's the modern relationship for a sexy woman: a sacred partnership meant to ignite the highest in each other, resulting in receiving all the attention and affection you can handle.

The modern way to give roses

Yes, sexy women tend to get lots of flowers given to them, yet they don't wait if he forgets. She expresses her self-worth and savors beauty with a beautiful bouquet of flowers for herself. Yet it doesn't stop here. After you buy twelve of your favorite flower, write down twelve ways you're a sexy woman, a great lover, a sultry goddess, a succulent wife, an off-the-charts mom, a gorgeous gift to humanity. Create this list and begin a healing ritual and joyous celebration of who you are TODAY. Sit yourself down and read each statement aloud as you put each exquisite stem into the vase, affirming how truly amazing you are.

This may sound corny, yet if you truly take it to heart and begin to offer love versus judgment to yourself your true confidence and radiance will illuminate your life. Then each time you gaze at the bouquet for the next week or more, you'll be reminded of how sexy and fabulous you are and as each flower opens and unfolds, you too will be inspired to open into your most luscious self for your pleasure and the pleasure of the one who gives you affection and attention, whether you've met him yet or not! He literally might be who you bump into when you leave your place to go for a walk that night and you're either open and juicy and unattached, having loved and celebrated yourself or you're all in your head, attached, trying to keep it together, and he doesn't even notice you. It's really that simple.

Get a sexy dress

I know that when I'm bloated, I don't feel the slightest bit sexy. Ditto right after my son was born, when I was carrying some extra weight. Ditto when I began menopause and my sweet body was adjusting. I had trouble shifting my thinking from "I'm fat" to "I'm voluptuous." I was withholding love to myself instead of giving it. I was turning off my light instead of shining it. I was closed to physical affection instead of open. I was hopeless, believing that I didn't deserve attention instead of welcoming it. When we're down on ourselves, it can be hard to pull ourselves out of a deep dark hole, so I say get a fabulous dress that looks good no matter what weight you're at! Perhaps find a wrap dress, as they are both sexy and feel good at the same time. Choose wonderful, exquisite fabrics that travel well and have designs that are slimming and flattering to many body shapes. The point is that we want to be able to have THAT DRESS that makes us feel fabulous whether we're ripped and in shape or need help feeling "voluptuous" (instead of bloated).

Get a great purse

When it comes right down to it, who am I to say that a purse is less spiritual than a priest's outfit? What I really think it comes down to is how you FEEL with it. If a great purse makes you shine from the inside out, makes you feel beautiful, radiant and luscious, then carry it. If you use the purse from an insecure place to get attention and feel enough, you'll never find a purse good enough to fill that empty hole. So I think it's brilliant if fashion can remind you that you are a light in this world. Take yourself out shopping for a hip, new purse (especially if you're like me and schlepped a diaper bag around for four years!). I love purses that include a light on the inside ... reminds you that YOU are a light in this world and to take time to go barefoot in the grass, snuggle by the fire and be thankful for the little things in life. (And it's practical to find your keys -- or condoms -- in the dark!)

Picnic in the driveway

I think it's sexy to plan a picnic for date night. It encourages snuggling, and laying on your side makes the outline of your body so voluptuous and your boobs look great! True or true? So know that you can plan a picnic for a sunset at the beach or at a look-out point or even if you're married you can have a picnic in the driveway in the back of your SUV! Can you imagine how shocked and pleased he'd be if he arrived home to see you all spread out on a big blanket and yummy pillows? In addition to some delicious food and beverages, bring something you have always dreamed of doing, some vacation catalogues, the calendar of music, sports, events or festivals in your city and plan some dates in the future. Watch a movie on the portable DVD player under the stars. Be sure to really savor your time together. Maybe even just listen. We women talk way more than men do. Make space to learn something about him you never knew and watch how he engulfs you in affections and appreciation for a special night.

DARK is good

Sometimes we're in go-go-go mode and don't feel in the mood to absolutely surrender into our feminine energy. And yet there's nothing sexy to him when we're in our masculine energy. Another way to make the shift into your feminine is to show your dark side ... with your heart open. Sometimes we need to inspire our men to take us in a more ravishing way than normal. Be willing to show him the way so he gets the hint. Remember that love is both dark and light. Light without love is flakey and shallow and doesn't penetrate your heart. Dark without love is cruel and you feel used, objectified, and even assaulted.

Yet light WITH love is profound, intense and blissful and extremely sensual and dark WITH love is ravishing, devouring, primal and intoxicating ... pure sexual ecstasy. Dark with loves means keeping your heart open, keeping aware of your intense love for this man, your primal attraction to him, while letting out your wild side. Never forget you are not just beautiful, you are Beauty Herself. You are not just sensual, you are Sensuality Herself. You are an amazing woman, a gift to your partner, friends, children and community. You are a sexy light in this world. Do all you can to shine fully by taking good care of yourself, taking time for yourself and letting your luscious, radiant sexuality wake up this world! And know that exactly who you are is gorgeous and perfect.

CHAPTER 12

SULTRY ON A BUDGET

"I feel sexy when I feel confident, when I'm sure of who I am, when I'm being true to myself."

- Debbie, 48

My final set of inspirations for your ultimate sexual expression has to do with being sexy on a shoe string. I want to abolish all misconceptions that being sexy requires limitless disposable income. It's not true. As you've learned in this book, sexy comes from the inside out. THEN a sexy woman expresses her sensuality on the outside through adornment of her gorgeous self and savoring delicious moments. This expression can be inexpensive or extravagant. It's more about WHO'S doing the spending, not WHAT you're spending on. Sexy is really a state of being and when you believe it, he does too and devours you and showers you with attention and affection.

PRACTICAL TIPS FOR THE SULTRY WOMAN
ON A BUDGET

Cleopatra's potluck

Join with your luscious friends and meet at one home in the evening. Dress like a goddess, bring decadent, sensual foods, put on some yummy music, lay around feeding each other by hand by candlelight and ONLY talk about what you're grateful for, what you think is sexy about each other, what you've savored this week about yourself, about life, about family, about career, what truly opened you up this week. You all know that what you focus on expands. Thinking about being broke attracts lack. Speaking and feeling grateful for what we have NOW while affirming what's sexy and fabulous about each other brings abundance and makes you feel full. You see, it would take no energy to go home after work that night, worry some, and avoid your feelings by eating too much or zoning out in front of the television or the computer. Yes, it will take some energy to make a meal, organize work/kids etc. to get to your friend's home, find a luscious outfit to wear, and be willing to curb unconscious talking and focus on gratitude, sensuality and empowering each other. And yet what you put in you get out tenfold. You might even curse me on the way over there and yet you will praise me, yourself and all your girlfriends as you drive home feeling full, alive and juicy.

Put it on the calendar to meet once a month and watch how your whole life becomes fuller. And yet don't necessarily wait until next month to fill yourself up. Perhaps you have roommates or a family that would love to eat dinner with your hands one night in a fort with flashlights while reciting all the reasons we can say "thank you" in our life. Sexy, sensual women always find ways to live a decadent life even on a budget.

Stained glass pedicure party

Again, find a night at one woman's home, each of you bring your three favorite color polishes, and one at a time, one woman's feet are bathed, massaged and painted in multiple colors by the group in a stained glass look. Tell her that like the multiple facets of a diamond, the multiple colors of her stained glass toes represent all the ways she is beautiful inside and out and how rich each of you feels to have a friend like her in your life. Tell her that every time she looks at her toes to remember that SHE makes people's lives rich.

Also, this is not a bad idea to ask of your man! My former husband allowed me and his nieces to paint his toes one day. It felt so naughty! You see, when you have one color, any little mistake shows, yet with multiple colors, people can make a total mess and then you simply clean up the edges and it's gorgeous. And remember, toes can be very erotic. Once yours are painted so uniquely it might be a great opportunity to ask your man to suck them, lick between the toes, massage firmly and completely turn you on!

Culture amidst the chaos

I love going out to plays and concerts, yet when you're on a budget it's difficult to rationalize that expenditure, and if you're like me, a part of my creativity and savoring of life dies. Not to worry? I'd bet glorious talent is as close as your backyard. Have a sexy friends night where each woman shares her talents, a dance, a song, a poem, a ritual. I was blown away on my birthday one year when I asked for no presents, instead, I asked for a gift of their creativity. I was in tears the whole time. Our friends are so talented! Remember, storytelling is an ancient way of passing along wisdom, so share what moves you in the nourishing safety of a candlelit living room of sensual women. Also, it's fun to ask your roommates, your man, or your kids to perform for you and create a throne for the queen to sit in, a crown to adorn her head as she watches -- perfect for you or your friends' birthday or a special occasion. It's these precious moments that create memories that last a lifetime. It takes a little courage, yet anything worth truly having quite often asks you to expand in order to receive. The bottom line with all this is when we're fully expressed in giving or receiving, we radiate pure sensuality and become enticing and attractive and more likely to receive affection.

Succulent swap and soiree

When you're on a budget, doesn't it make you want new clothes even more? I remember in my leaner times that everything in my closet seemed particularly dull, old and frumpy when I was on a budget. I'm not into whiners so this is what I've done in the past: clean out your closets of anything that doesn't scream sexy goddess, meet at one woman's home, turn up the heat, shut the drapes and turn the living room into a chic boudoir changing room! Pour wine or tea, play music and try on new looks from your friends' hand-me-downs. Practice being comfortable changing in front of your girlfriends! Have some fun and with kindness and humor, let each tell the truth. "That looks amazing on you!" "You're smokin' hot!" or "If you walk out that door wearing that we may have to kill you. Bad. Wrong. Take it off."

Take the clothes that are left over to Goodwill. You'll feel stunning and lavish in your new wardrobe. You'll look into your closet now and see outfits that encourage you to love your sensual body. AND you'll feel abundant and grateful as you give to those less fortunate.

Re-gifting the kids

Many moms complain that they haven't had a date night in forever because they don't want to spend money on a night out AND on the sitter. Point taken. So here's what I'd do: Package up your precious ones and gift them to family or friends for nap time, bedtime, or even just playtime. Literally drop them off with bows on their heads so that they don't feel rejected – instead they feel like a present to someone! Then make YOU the present as you await your hunky man to arrive home while you're unwinding in a hot, relaxing bubble bath, complete with a big ol' bow on your head. Yes, you ARE a present! When your kids return, you will feel so much more grateful for them because you've recharged your batteries.

Boycott the coffee house

What I mean here is that you might want to see how much you spend on lattes in a month and instead go buy some decadent bath products. Instead of eating out so much you could go to a gourmet market and buy some fabulous cheeses and insanely fabulous bread. Instead of getting something new once a week at a chain clothing store, wait three months and go buy that off-the-charts designer outfit that makes you feel like a million bucks. A sign of a sexy woman is that she's in pleasure with life. Check in to see if you are feeling drab thinking you can't afford something divine when you could alter your spending habits and truly savor a decadent product fit for a succulent queen like yours.

CHAPTER 13

WHEN MAMA'S HAPPY

"I feel sexy when I've accomplished a full day of work, giving myself to others. It's a soul thing, my whole body feels sensuous."

- Claire, 44

How many of you reading this are moms? Or are moms to your men? Or are moms to your careers? Or are mothers to your own life journey? We all have the mother archetype in us and these are some great ideas to go with the flow and have some fun as we mother ourselves, our lives, our communities. The following tips are creative, fun ways to bring out your inner child, whether you have youngsters to inspire or girlfriends to play with who are young at heart.

BEING A GREAT CARETAKER OF YOUR LIFE, YOUR CAREER, YOUR FAMILY

While there's a tendency to put dead people on pedestals, I really did have an amazing mom. She was sexy and used to lie draped across the couch in her pink velour robe, scarf on her head, horn rimmed glasses, watching my every move as I balanced the

Fisher-Price people on my three speed Fisher-Price record player. She made a point of doing cool things with us before we were five ... go on a one-car ferry, go to a cattle auction (you can tell I'm from rural Canada), go to Vancouver Island every spring break to hunt for crabs, finger paint in shaving cream on our old, burnt orange 70's kitchen table. But who in the world has an ounce of creativity left when we're operating on fumes? I know I used to resort to putting on a video for my son just to give myself time to have a shower some mornings. Would you like to know how I turned things around and now we dance on the coffee table and have picnics in the driveway with the sun setting on our happy faces?

We Never Get There So Go With the Flow

I think a great caretaker of children, of our mates, of our careers, and of our sanity knows how to find balance moment to moment. Just like the journey is really the destination, balance is not to be found, only experienced in the moment. Same as love is never captured, only given and received moment to moment.

"Once you realize that the road is the goal and that you are always on the road, not to reach a goal, but to enjoy its beauty and its wisdom, life ceases to be a task and becomes natural and simple, in itself an ecstasy."

- Sri Nisargadatta Mahara

Given that there's no outcome of parenting really, just the moment-to-moment embracing of experiences, then I don't have to do it perfectly. If discipline is called for, GREAT. And if silliness is called for I can be silly, too. For me, being a great caretaker is being present to what my son needs, what I need, what WE need for this moment to be its best. I have wasted so much energy trying to control the moment. We have swim class to get to NOW. We were planning on going to the chiropractor NOW. It's summer and he HAS to wear shorts. It's July and we DON'T watch Polar Express until Christmas. Just who is coming up with all these rules? Me. And who is deciding to resist my son's enthusiasm for the moment? Yep, me again. Of course there are structures, deadlines, rules and appropriateness that I adhere to so that he can operate successfully in society, but will it kill him (or more honestly kill me) if he wears his Super Man costume to the grocery store with me?

A decade ago, as I was trying to get him to preschool NOW he was down near the end of the drive way and I screamed, "SEAT! NOW!" Exasperated he screamed back, "Mom, I'm looking at the world!" That stopped me in my tracks. What was twenty to thirty seconds more to look at the sky, the birds, the house across the street, the cars, whatever he saw? Once I joined him, let him show me his world, we easily got in the car and I told him I didn't like to get angry and asked how could I be a better mom. He told me, "Relax." Point taken. And the real point taken is that I now have extra energy to be sexy, take care of me, and find creative things to do with him. Yes, whenever we get "there," "here" we are again, so let's relax and enjoy the crisis and go with the flow in our families, in our careers, in our relationships and in our minds.

Read these suggestions as joyful things to do with your children, your mate, your girlfriends, all meant to fill you up from the inside out to radiate your true sensual nature of savoring moments. In fact I have an entire awesome book for moms called **When Mama's Happy, Everybody's Happy~ The Missing Handbook to Motherhood** available on my site www.AllanaPratt.com and Amazon.com.

15 SEXY MOM SOLUTIONS

1. **Guitars on the front porch** – Why play inside when you can offer the neighborhood a concert? It really makes us feel like we're a band when we open the door as if the curtain is rising and we're willing to look and sound silly and sing full out.

2. **Dancing on the coffee table** – I have a super sturdy, huge coffee table that, when upon it, one can see perfectly into the mirror over the fireplace. So why not rock out to kids' music or the reggae song "One Love".

3. **Bouncing on balls in the exercise room** – One way I used to get my workout in was to allow my son to climb up behind me on the big exercise ball, hold his hands and we bounce to his favorite songs, work out my thighs and pretend we're doing a concert.

4. **Wash the truck and water fight** – Who doesn't love a clean vehicle and a great water fight? Enlist the boyfriend or hubby, and getting all wet's pretty sexy.

5. **The tramp** – I love the trampoline for being crazy and free and also bouncing and relaxing my tense body. I used to wear myself out and lay there under the huge sky with my little man or my boyfriend, suspended and floating above the Earth.

6. **Drawing on the steps** – Words carry energy, so we've always written on our front steps in chalk, "Welcome to the house of love, joy and strawberries" (my son used to help with content). We also painted the cement in the back yard with washable paints, and I wrote affirmations. One summer we pretended we were Cirque Du Soleil dancers and painted our bodies, too.

7. **Polar Express in June** – Yes, I gave in, all those years ago I made hot chocolate and got out the huge box the fake Christmas tree came in (which reminded my son of a train

car), and we snuggled in with blankets and watched Polar Express. He still remembers it.

8. **Prayers and candles at the dinner table** – Rituals really help you become present, sensually savoring moments. We used to light candles every night at dinner. We had a rudimentary prayer of "Thank you for food, family, friends and fun." When we blew out the candles we made wishes for ourselves and then for others with the extra candles. This could be instantly spiced up if you're dining with your lover … I wish that you'd tie me up.

9. **The matching game for dinner time** – I'm big on discipline and manners and yet I balance it out with fun so we used to have regular picnics at sunset in the driveway with blankets, pillows and his favorite matching the cards game. Sometimes people who walked by after dinner would stop and help out. Hysterical.

10. **Meditation time together** – Remember when I said my son couldn't come into my room until "seven zero zero"? Well, one morning he broke the rule and I was meditating and I simply said he could join me to meditate or go back in his room. I couldn't believe it – he joined me. I was chanting Sanskrit and he loved it. For years every so often, he's come in and want me to chant for him. How divine.

11. **Reading and Jujitsu in bed** – Some mornings we had to get off to school, yet I loved the mornings when we read together and then he attacked me with his Jujitsu moves and we'd wrestle.

12. **Thank you's and songs at bedtime** – I wanted to teach my son about gratitude — that what you focus on expands — and yet I also wanted to teach him to embrace even the challenges, learn the lessons and let it all go versus holding onto grudges. So each night we'd say our "Thank you's"

and I'd help him to be grateful for everything the Universe provided to expand and open us.

13. **All about pleasure** – After a long day of work or mothering it's important that we make room to nourish ourselves with pleasure. I'm officially drinking half coffee and half "teachino" filled with my Shaman Shack herbs … and it's my ritual to make a cup and wind down on the porch. Also one night I was so horny that I wanted to use my vibrator and my batteries had died so I hijacked some from my son's toy. Please. Haven't you done that? A girl's got to do what a girl's got to do!

14. **Fears about my life** – Another way to use your downtime to your advantage is to face your fears instead of getting stuck on email all night. If something's bothering you, your luscious radiance is at risk, so call that friend, have that cry, talk to a coach, journal until you find clarity. Sexy women are courageous and go to their depths until they find peace and clarity.

15. **Dance it out at night** – Once my son was in bed, I'd light candles and dance out my frustrations, and I'd dance out my tears of being lonely, of yearning for my lover. Sexy women aren't impermeable. Every woman gets scared, angry and afraid. It's just that sexy women bravely feel, process and release their feelings so that they're once again tapped into the juicy energy in their body and shining open to the world.

And any moms who are reading this, please know I celebrate, honor and value all that you do for your family! Tell me something. When the day is go–go-go and you were there for everyone, were you as playful as you'd have liked? As patient as you knew you could be? Alive enough to enjoy a beautiful love-making session that night? Or were you exhausted because you put everyone else in front of you, again?

The guilt that rises up in we moms is intense. Saying "No" to others instead of "Yes" to ourselves can be excruciatingly challenging sometimes. Frankly I don't want to say "no" to my son, and yet I know I'm operating on fumes. I know YOU know that filling up YOUR tank is crucial for you to enjoy the journey of motherhood because all too soon, they're grown! Grab that book I mentioned, **When Mama's Happy Everybody's Happy** ... or give yourself some human connection with my Intimacy Success Advisor on an Intimacy Blindspot Breakthrough Call to help you feel safe, heard and discover the block that's separating you from your happy place. I chose to be the space in which my child flourished and I learned to ask for help every step of the way.

WE need to take care of ourselves so we can be who we want to be for those we love.

YOU DESERVE IT!!

CONCLUSION

WEAVING IT ALL TOGETHER INTO THE TAPESTRY CALLED YOU!

You've taken in a tremendous amount of information. My recommendation would be not to have any huge expectations of yourself of how sexy you need to feel by next Thursday. Don't give up if you don't get all the affection you desire by the end of the week. Know that you're on a journey, you've done beautifully up 'til now and you will continue to unfold into the gorgeous goddess you are more quickly and easily now that you have this information. Remember that everyone has bad days so instead remember to savor and focus on your good days. Cherish and treasure yourself over and above anything else.

What I find is that when I do my sensuality practices to make him show up, he takes forever. Yet when I'm willing to do my sensuality practices for ME, all of my dreams show up more quickly, effortlessly and in unexpected, beautiful ways. Remember your sexiness is the gift the Universe gave you in being a woman. Every single one of us has it inside. No one is left out. It's a part of you. And YOU are a gift to enjoy, to savor and to gift to the world.

So here's what I invite you to do next:

Check in with your body right now. How do you feel having read this book, listened to this book? Better? More seen, heard, validated, inspired, empowered, guided and celebrated? What would it be like to feel that more often? What would it be like to talk to me personally twice a month to ask your questions and receive guidance, sisterhood and support on your journey? What would it be like to receive practical and pleasure-filled interviews and powerful, guided meditations to help you heal your heart and let go of control and inspiring video tips with additional practices to keep you balanced?

Well, there's all of that and more in my Heartmates for Singles (with Dating App) or Couples at www.AllanaPratt.com. And there's the opportunity to work with me in my Intimacy Breakthrough Group Coaching Program, Inner Circle or Private VIP Intensives. You can learn more AND discover your intimacy blindspot on an Intimacy Blindspot Breakthrough Call at www.AllanaPratt.com.

Please remember being sexy, classy, sensual and magnetic isn't a goal, it's a way of being. Once you've found your partner, you'll want to KEEP them and grow together more deeply over time, so these practices will support you in each phase of your relationship, help you to feel more confident, luscious and empowered as a woman, while giving you tools to take your relationship deeper so that he claims you and adores you to your core.

And just because being sexy, sensual, and classy is a capacity you lose if you don't stay conscious and practicing, don't think of it as one more thing to do.

Think of it as something you GET to do. It's your birthright to shine your full radiance, to live your most successful life, to enjoy a deeply passionate relationship and to be at peace with exactly who you are.

You are never alone!

You are officially a part of my sisterhood.

You are in my heart forever.

I am inspired by your courage.

I am amazed at your beauty.

I am honored to serve you.

I wish you deep rest into the most luscious, dark, deep, moist, powerful parts of you ... and may you effortlessly shine in this world ... drenched in attention ... and showered in affection by men worthy of your grandeur.

You are Sensuality Herself.

Dear glorious Sister ... soar, shine and be free!

All my love,

Allana

A BIT ABOUT ME

Even though the accent's basically gone, I'm a small-town Canadian girl who loves big-hearted guys with sexy trucks, Crispy Crunch chocolate bars, and nourishing walks in the woods. I was raised by a teacher mother and pharmacist father who divorced when I was 18. While I enjoyed magical summers at the lake, most of my school years were spent feeling misunderstood for my expression, my enthusiasm, my quirks and my (overly) sensitive heart.

With encouragement from both my grandmothers, I found the courage at 19 years old to hop on my Uncle Phil's 18-wheeler semi to live my dreams in Hollywood. While I was brave enough and talented enough, I didn't have a work visa so the only job I could find, rather than go home and accept failure, was in Japan.

That Japan work became four years as a successful model, dancer and spokesperson on television, doing magazine covers, billboards, movies, music videos and runways. It was there I chose to dance as a showgirl, learning for the first time to no longer see my body as a piece of meat, but a sacred work of art capable of awakening nobility in a man, and radiance in a woman. I came to truly embody the beauty and sacredness of my erotic nature.

I arrived in Japan with $40 to my name and my Dad's Visa to be used only if I "was ready to stop these shenanigans". Didn't happen.

Home sweet home began as a cockroach-infested shack shared with fourteen other foreigners. By year four I was making more money than both my parents combined and having way more fun than I ever thought possible. It was there I met my first husband: a tall, dark, and handsome multimillionaire. I followed him to New York City where we married.

I graduated cum laude from Columbia University and interned at CNN, yet I was dying inside because I had decided his net worth made him more worthy than me. While I loved him, in hindsight I don't really think I knew what love was because I didn't deeply love myself yet. I was afraid to pass up such a picture-perfect life. My wounded self-worth asked, *Will anyone this well off ever love me again?* My limited self-esteem was dissolving, so when people asked, "What KIND of dancer were you?" I lied, hid and drowned in shame and guilt about what once had brought me great freedom, joy and sacred empowerment. I desired being a more authentic and empowered woman, and the relationship was no longer a fit. After therapy and workshops didn't change anything, I divorced him.

A few years later, I had bought my own condo in the South Bay of Los Angeles and was working as a Pilates instructor and life coach. I was struggling to make a new tumultuous relationship work with a charismatic, passionate (read as, angry) guy, when I found out my mom had cancer. It all happened so fast. She called me to say she was too tired to fight, and in ten traumatic yet beautiful days … she was gone.

The next weekend I got pregnant at my sister's wedding. Since I couldn't save mom, I tried to save the relationship with Mr. Anger Issues. I take full responsibility that I didn't marry for love, rather after shutting my heart down, I married for the desperate semblance of security. I thought a child would fill the void in my Soul. It's no shocker that this ended in divorce and there I was … a single, motherless mom, retreating inside the home that I had renovated with my inheritance, only to later sell it in debt, feeling ashamed and forgotten by the Universe.

I hit rock bottom.

The journey to regain my confidence, succulence and self-love has become my delicious life's work, being a transparent leader to my clients and community, returning to the life force creative energy found in both our pleasure, joy, and bliss and in our wobbly vulnerability and don't-fuck-with-me potency. I have a flourishing relationship with my son and choose to honor his choice to live at his Dads. I pinch myself regularly that I GET to dive deep and love people for my job as an Intimacy Expert.

OTHER PRODUCTS BY ALLANA

FOR WOMEN:

How to Be and Stay Sexy

https://allanapratt.com/product/how-to-be-and-stay-sexy/

When Mama's Happy, Everybody's Happy

https://allanapratt.com/product/when-mamas-happy-everybodys-happy/

Thriving Intimacy for Her, 35 Days of Guided Meditations, Audio

https://allanapratt.com/product/thriving-intimacy-guided-meditations/

FOR MEN:

Scoring a Relationship

https://allanapratt.com/product/scoring-a-relationship/

How to Be a Noble Badass

https://allanapratt.com/product/how-to-be-a-noble-badass/

Thriving Intimacy for Him, 35 Days of Guided Meditations, Audio

https://allanapratt.com/product/thriving-intimacy-guided-meditations-for-him

FOR BOTH:

Finding 'The One 'Is Bullsh*t -BECOMING 'The One' is Brilliant & Beautiful

https://allanapratt.com/product/finding-the-one-is-bs-becoming-the-one-is-brilliant-beautiful/

HeartMates Dating App & Intimacy Training

www.HeartMates.app

Printed in Great Britain
by Amazon